Regulatory Freedom and Investment Treaty Arbitration

International Investment Law and Arbitration

The titles published in this series are listed at *brill.com/rpias*

Regulatory Freedom and Investment Treaty Arbitration

By

Aniruddha Rajput

BRILL | NIJHOFF

LEIDEN | BOSTON

The Library of Congress Cataloging-in-Publication Data is available online at https://catalog.loc.gov
LC record available at https://lccn.loc.gov/2026934322

Typeface for the Latin, Greek, and Cyrillic scripts: "Brill". See and download: brill.com/brill-typeface.

ISSN 2405-576X
ISBN 978-90-04-75976-3 (paperback)
ISBN 978-90-04-75983-1 (e-book)
DOI 10.1163/9789004759831

For Maa, Dada and Anahita

Contents

CHAPTER 1

Introduction

Expectations from States – being a repository of public interest – to undertake multitude of regulations are on a rise. Through the exercise of the sovereign 'right to regulate' or 'regulatory freedom', States are expected to tackle wide-ranging global and national problems, such as climate change, human rights, labour standards, protection of health, provision for appropriate quality of food, water and sanitation. The inventory of the challenges faced domestically and internationally have steadily risen and it is doubtful if they will recede anytime soon. Even from a theoretical perspective, the characterization of the 'State' as a legal entity, based on the functions it is expected to perform has majorly transformed. In the early phases, the State was characterized as a laissez-faire State, where the role of the State was minimal and limited to internal and external security and international relations.[1] The occasions and expectations of regulatory exercises were limited, if not entirely absent. With the expansion of the challenges and the regulatory functions expected of the State to perform, the State transformed into a 'welfare' State. The State and its organs, particularly the government started participating in socio-economic activities. The limbs of the State, particularly the government was no more a bystander anymore. It entered key industries dealing primarily with public utility services and natural resources-based industries; sometimes even in many other sectors.[2] In its present form, which is complex, the State continues to perform the activities of a welfare State through its engagement with some micro-economic activities but its overall participation as an actor in the markets has relatively reduced. The focus has shifted on being an umpire, and setting rules of conduct and overseeing compliance. This activity requires actively making, changing and overseeing implementation of regulations. Therefore, the contemporary form of the State is termed as the 'regulatory' State.[3] The governance models existing today comprise of different features

1 Sidney Fine, *Laissez Faire and the General-Welfare State; A Study of Conflict in American Thought, 1865–1901* (USA: University of Michigan, 1956).

2 See Martin Loughlin & Colin Scott, "The Regulatory State" in *Developments in British Politics*, ed. Patrick Dunleavy, Andrew Gamble, Ian Holliday & Gillian Peele (Basingstoke: Macmillan Press, 1997); Karen Yeung, "Regulatory State" in *The Oxford Handbook of Regulation*, ed. Robert Baldwin, Martin Cave & Martin Lodge (New York: Oxford University Press, 2010), pp. 65–6.

3 David Osborne & Ted Gaebler, *Reinventing Government: How the Entrepreneurial Spirit is Transforming the Public Sector* (USA: Addision Wesley, 1992), p. 25; Karen Yeung, "Regulatory

 | DOI:10.1163/9789004759831_002

combined in diverse degree of a welfare State and a regulatory State. The framing of regulations and performing regulatory activities has taken a central role despite sometimes the State continues to be a participant in the economic activity like other private participants.[4] The present-day regulatory State undertakes multifarious tasks ranging across diverse areas that affect different areas of public and private life.

Pressures from different stakeholders, both domestic and international operate as additional driving forces for States to exercise regulatory freedom extensively and innovatively.[5] People and non-governmental organizations (NGOs) hold States responsible for failing to keep up with these regulatory expectations. States are being seen as a trustee or an agency responsible to ensure and achieve community interests.[6] Within the State, other organs of State such as legislatures put pressure on the governments to act and the judiciary holds the government accountable for non-satisfaction of regulatory expectations.[7] Various international commitments that State undertake through binding treaty obligations and other soft law demands that States voluntarily decide to implement require exercise of regulatory freedom. The underlying motives of regulatory exercises are non-economic considerations – particularly public interest concerns.

State" in *The Oxford Handbook of Regulation*, ed. Robert Baldwin, Martin Cave & Martin Lodge (New York: Oxford University Press, 2010), pp. 66–7.

4 Giandomenico Majone, "The Rise of the Regulatory State in Europe" *West European Politics* 17 (1994): 77–101; Giandomenico Majone, "From the Positive to the Regulatory State: Causes and Consequences of Changes in the Modern Governance" *Journal of Public Policy* 17, no. 2 (1997): 139–168.

5 Robert Baldwin, Martin Cave & Martin Lodge, "Introduction: Regulation – The Field and the Developing Agenda" in *The Oxford Handbook of Regulation*, ed. Robert Baldwin, Martin Cave & Martin Lodge (New York: Oxford University Press, 2010), pp. 6–8.

6 Eyal Benvenisti, "Trust" *American Journal of International Law* 107, no. 2 (2013): 295–348; Georg Nolte and Eyal Benvenisti, "International Law and Trust" *American Journal of International Law* 112, no. 3 (2018): 345–378; Bruno Simma, "Community Interests in International Law" *European Journal of International Law* 11, no. 2 (2001): 233–263; Emmanuel Gaillard and Donald T. Trautman, "Trusts in Non-Trust Countries: Conflict of Laws and the Hague Convention on Trusts" *The American Journal of Comparative Law* 35, no. 2 (Spring 1987): 307–340; Matthew Harding, "Trust and Fiduciary Law" *Oxford Journal of Legal Studies* 33, no. 1 (Spring 2013): 81–102.

7 A major area on rise is the climate change litigation where proceedings have been brought successfully before municipal courts to force governments to do more to tackle climate change. See *Urgenda v the Netherlands Urgenda Foundation v. State of the Netherlands*, ECLI:NL:RBDHA:2015:7196 (Hague District Court 2015).; "Climate litigation more than doubles in five years, now a key tool in delivering climate justice" UNEP, accessed 30 April 2024, https://www.unep.org/news-and-stories/press-release/climate-litigation-more-doubles-five-years-now-key-tool-delivering.

Regulatory measures – whether in response to urgent or long-term concerns – are bound to affect businesses and investors: foreign and domestic alike. Speaking of climate change – the largest contemporary challenge faced by humanity – climate change agreements, which most States are bound by, require drastic measures including major changes to the structure and functioning of the economy and financial flows. It would be impossible for States to undertake regulations to implement these obligations if States were to compensate for every loss suffered as a result of the measures undertaken to implement climate change obligations. Especially since the measures of the State would be taken to uphold and protect public interest at the national as well as international level. Lowe points out that States cannot be expected to buy back their regulatory powers by compensating for each loss arising out of a regulatory measure.[8]

A domestic investor would have few alternatives except approaching national courts, where the likelihood of beneficial regulations adopted in public interest being upheld, especially considering the seriousness and magnitude of the issue sought to be regulated, is high. The same cannot be said of foreign investors. States have entered into international investment agreements (IIAs) in the form of bilateral investment treaties (BITs), investment chapters in free trade agreements (FTAs) and multilateral treaties providing investment protection such as the Energy Charter Treaty (ECT). IIAs have opened the avenue for challenging sovereign actions before an international tribunal based on treatment standards in an IIA and public international law. Moreover, treatment standards are flexible and amenable to broad discretionary interpretations by arbitral tribunals, thereby, narrowing the scope for exercising regulatory freedom for States. Technically, only foreign investors are entitled to invoke investment arbitration but with the possibility of restructured investments and double nationality, investments ultimately held for the benefit of a national may even qualify as investments for protection under investment treaties.[9]

Therefore, a major doctrinal challenge in international investment law is the relationship between the demands of public interest to be achieved through exercise of regulatory freedom by States and the limits placed by IIAs through treatment standards. Whether States can make and change

---

8 Vaughan Lowe, "Regulation or Expropriation?" *Current Legal Problems* 55 (2002): 447, 451.

9 See Marc-Antoine Couet, "Round-Tripping in International Investment Law: A Teleological Assessment" *The Journal of World Investment & Trade*, 22, no. 3, 459–501 and Javier García Olmedo, "Claims by Dual Nationals under Investment Treaties: Are Investors Entitled to Sue Their Own States?" *Journal of International Dispute Settlement* (2017): pp. 1–33.

regulations in public interest on the one hand, and on the other whether foreign investors that commit their capital for a long duration in a State and undertake the business risk can be protected from arbitrary, unreasonable, and discriminatory measures. If States are required to pay compensation for each measure adopted in public interest that has a negative economic impact on the foreign investor, it would generate 'regulatory chill' and dissuade States from taking necessary and urgent actions. But if all actions of States are justified under the rubric of public interest, then what remains of the protection under the IIAs? The central theme of this contribution is to look at the relationship between regulatory freedom and investment treaty arbitration. States do not lose regulatory freedom by entering into treaties because regulatory freedom is a right emanating from customary international law. However, the right is not absolute and subject to restrictions under customary international law. If the measures of States wall within those limitations they would not breach treatment standards under IIAs.

Regulatory freedom or right to regulate represents the discretion of States to undertake regulations. Regulations are a broad range of actions taken by governments to achieve a particular purpose.[10] These actions are referred to as 'measures' in international investment law. If not always, some IIAs define a measure to cover the broad range of actions that governments might take.[11]

10 *Suez, Sociedad General de Aguas de Barcelona, S.A. and Vivendi Universal, S.A. v Argentine Republic*, ICSID Case No. ARB/03/19, Decision on Liability (30 June 2010), para. 131.

11 Model Agreement Between Canada and [...] for the Promotion and Protection of Investments (2021), Government of Canada, 12 May 2021, https://www.international.gc.ca/trade-commerce/trade-agreements-accords-commerciaux/agr-acc/fipa-apie/2021_model_fipa-2021_modele_apie.aspx?lang=eng; Article 1, Treaty Between the Government of the United States of America and the Government of [country] concerning the encouragement an reciprocal protection of investment, 2012, https://ustr.gov/sites/default/files/BIT%20text%20for%20ACIEP%20Meeting.pdf; Agreement for the reciprocal promotion and protection of investments between Colombia and France, 10 July 2014, accessed June 29 2024, https://investmentpolicy.unctad.org/international-investment-agreements/treaties/bilateral-investment-treaties/3488/colombia---france-bit-2014-; Germany–Iraq Bilateral Investment Treaty 2010, accessed June 29 2024, https://investmentpolicy.unctad.org/international-investment-agreements/treaties/bilateral-investment-treaties/1693/germany---iraq-bit-2010-; Republic of Korea–Serbia Bilateral Investment Treaty 2023, accessed June 29, 2024, https://investmentpolicy.unctad.org/international-investment-agreements/treaties/bilateral-investment-treaties/5080/korea-republic-of---serbia-bit-2023-; UNCTAD, "Japan – International Investment Agreements," accessed June 29 2024, https://investmentpolicy.unctad.org/international-investment-agreements/countries/105/japan; Agreement between the Republic of Colombia and the Kingdom of Spain for the Promotion and Reciprocal Protection of Investments, 16 September 2021, accessed June 29 2024, https://investmentpolicy.unctad.org/international-investment-agreements/treaties/bilateral-investment-treaties/4976/colombia---spain-bit-2021-.

Regulations are a result not just of governmental actions but also of legislative actions of a State. However, it would be inappropriate to categorize adjudicative actions of the judiciary as regulations.

The approach of investment tribunals has evolved overtime. After initial reluctance to accommodate regulatory freedom and its direct or indirect rejection, tribunals have been deferential towards legitimate regulatory measures. There are several conceptual issues that remain outstanding and insufficiently explained. The tendency is to look 'inside' the IIAs to find if there is regulatory freedom and the conclusions arrived are that there is either very little or no regulatory freedom and then suggestions are made to change treaties and expressly add regulatory freedom.[12] Or, efforts are made to secure regulatory freedom by suggesting that investment tribunals should grant greater deference to avoid States from being held responsible for breach of IIAs.[13] This contribution takes an 'external' view that is it looks outside of IIAs and investigates the manner in which regulatory freedom is treated despite the presence of treaty obligations in public international law. It may not, however, be correct to call this view 'external' because IIAs are creatures of international law; they operate within the sphere of and are bound by the rules of international law. Positive international law is sufficiently equipped to look at this relationship and there is no need to turn to policy suggestions to balance regulatory freedom with treatment standards. The addition of provisions into treaties to protect regulatory freedom does not mean that regulatory freedom under customary international law is ineffective.

Due to the conceptual closeness between regulatory freedom and indirect expropriation and the way this relationship has unfolded in investment arbitrations the early development of the law in investment arbitration cases focused on regulatory freedom in relation to indirect expropriation. As the cases have progressed, tribunals have discussed the relationship between regulatory freedom and other treatment standards, particularly the fair and equitable treatment standard. The principles regulating the relationship between regulatory freedom and each of the treatment standards are peculiar and influenced by the contents of the treatment standard. Those peculiarities and the

12 Catherine Titi, *Right to Regulate in International Investment Law* (Nomos, 2014); Yulia Levashova, *The Right of States to Regulate in International Investment Law: The Search for Balance Between Public Interest and Fair and Equitable Treatment* (Kluwer Law International, 2019).

13 Caroline Henckels, *Proportionality and Deference in Investor-State Arbitration: Balancing Investment Protection and Regulatory Autonomy* (Cambridge University Press, 2015); Lone Wandahl Mouyal, *International Investment Law and the Right to Regulate: A Human Rights Perspective* (Routledge, 2016).

relationship of regulatory freedom with prominent treatment standards are the object of enquiry of the present contribution. Most importantly the decisions of other international courts and tribunals are a source of inspiration and guidance since they have looked extensively at customary international law and its relationship with treaty obligations, which is at the core of the relationship between regulatory freedom and investment treaty arbitration.

This introduction (Chapter I) is followed by Chapter II which explores the nature of regulatory freedom in international law. In doctrinal international law, at the conceptual level, regulatory freedom is an integral part of sovereignty and one of the multiple facets of sovereignty. Equally, regulatory freedom satisfies the requirements of customary international law. This chapter explores both the aspects: conceptual and the procedure for establishing customary international law and argues that regulatory freedom is a rule of customary international law. Chapter III introduces the relationship between regulatory freedom and treatment standards at the general level as interaction of 'norms'. Regulatory freedom and treatment standards are based in two distinct sources of international law: customary international law and treaty respectively. Consequentially, their interaction is regulated by the principles governing interaction between customary international law and treaty. Treaties do no exclude the operation of customary international law, unless there is clear and sufficient indication. A treaty norm may supersede a customary norm if they are in 'conflict' with one another. It is argued in this chapter that the situation of conflict of a treaty and customary norm does not exist in the case with regulatory freedom and treatment standards. The general discussion on the level of norms in Chapter III serves as a framework for a granular discussion on the interaction between regulatory freedom and specific treatment standards to investigate whether and how States retain regulatory freedom in light of the treatment standards. Chapter IV discusses the effect of indirect expropriation on regulatory freedom. Chapter V discusses the effect of the fair and equitable treatment (FET). Thereafter, Chapter VI elaborates the elements of regulatory freedom: namely *bona fide* or good faith; non-discrimination and public interest. This chapter also presents the discussion on the influence of most favoured nation (MFN) and national treatment (NT) influence the understanding of non-discrimination, which is an element of regulatory freedom. Chapter VII discusses the standard of review applied by investment tribunals and the appropriateness of those standards for review of regulatory freedom. The standards of review applied by tribunals is inconsistent and this contribution argues that a good faith review is the most appropriate standard. Finally, Chapter VIII provides conclusions.

CHAPTER 2

Regulatory Freedom – A Customary International Law Rule

Regulatory freedom has also been referred in the classical international law literature as 'police powers'.[1] The word 'police' may create the misimpression that it is related to policing and maintenance of law and order or limited to law enforcement. In the classical literature, police powers was used to connote the prerogative of the government to regulate activities within its jurisdiction and perform other regulatory functions beyond mere policing.[2] The word police has always been connected with 'policy' throughout the genesis and evolution of the term police powers. Therefore, police powers signifies the policies adopted by a State.[3] Adam Smith expressed police power as "the theory of the general principles of law and government" including all regulations of a country in relation to trade, commerce, agriculture, and manufacturing belong to the regulatory power of the State.[4]

Black's Law Dictionary defines police powers in the most comprehensive manner:

> The inherent and plenary power of a sovereign to make all laws necessary and proper to preserve the public security, order, health, morality, and justice. It is a fundamental power essential to government, and it cannot be surrendered by the legislature or irrevocably transferred away from government.[5]

1 For a discussion on the evolution of the concept see Aniruddha Rajput, *Regulatory Freedom and Indirect Expropriation in Investment Arbitration* (Kluwer International, 2018), pp. 9–11.

2 Santiago Legarre, "The Historical Background of the Police Power" *Journal of Constitutional Law* 9, no. 3 (2007): 745, 761–762 (citing *Chambers Dictionary of Etymology*, ed. Robert K Barnhart, (1988), 812–813).

3 Joseph Worcester, *Worcester's Academic Dictionary: A New Etymological Dictionary of the English Language* (Philadelph J.B. Lippincott Company, 1910), 421.

4 R.L. Meek, D.D. Raphael & Peter Stein, ed., *Lectures on Jurisprudence by Adam Smith* (Oxford: Clarendon Press, 1978), 398, 586.

5 Bryan Garner, *Black's Law Dictionary*, 10th ed. (United States of America: Thomson Reuters, 2014), 1345.

 | DOI:10.1163/9789004759831_003

Both Grotious and Vattel treated police powers as the authority of the State to undertake measures in public interest without being responsible for harm caused to private persons and entities.[6] Acknowledging the wide power to regulate economic affairs and affect private property in public interest, Vattel said:

> It must also be observed, that individuals are not free in the economy or government of their affairs as not to be subject to the regulations of polity, made by the sovereign. For instance, if vines are greatly multiplied in a country, which is in want of corn, the sovereign may forbid the planting of the vine in fields proper for tillage, for here the public welfare and the safety of the state are concerned. When a reason of such importance requires it, the sovereign, or the magistrate, may oblige an individual to sell all the provisions that are more than sufficient for the subsistence of his family, and fix the price. The public authority may and ought to hinder monopolies, and suppress all practices tending to raise the price of provisions.[7]

However, a State is not protected if it causes deliberate harm. The exercise of police powers is subject to the limits of "prudential considerations".[8] Any "ill-considered, hasty or even discriminatory impositions" are not covered by police powers.[9] Thus, the presence of a harm arising out of the acts of the State so described in the preceding sentences takes the measure out of the definition of police powers.

In contemporary international law, regulatory freedom that is police powers has attained the status of customary international law. Regulatory freedom is an integral part of sovereignty, which is in turn is a rule of customary international law. Therefore, conceptually it is on safe grounds to suggest that regulatory freedom is a rule of customary international law by virtue of being an aspect of sovereignty. Additionally, there is sufficient evidence to establish that regulatory freedom satisfies the requirements to become a rule of customary international law.

---

6 Hugo Grotius, Chapter II, De Jure Belli Et Pacis, Book II, (1625), para. XIX; Emerde Vattel, Chapter VIII, The Law of Nations Book I, (1758), para. 88.

7 Emerichde Vattel, Le Droit Des Gens, Ou Principles De La Naturelle, Appliques a La Conduit Et Aux Affaires Des Nations Et Des Souvrains, Book I (London, Newbery et al. 1759–1760), 104.

8 Santiago Legarre, "The Historical Background of the Police Power" *Journal of Constitutional Law* 9, no. 3 (2007): 812–13 (see n. 15).

9 Joseph Sax, "Takings and the Police Power" *Yale Law Journal* (1964): 36, 57.

1 Regulatory Freedom an Aspect of Sovereignty

Sovereignty is a multi-faceted concept in positive international law and regulatory freedom is one of the aspects of is. Sovereignty is a defining characteristic a State and distinguishes it from other entities. It is a 'personified legal order' which is a collective representation of the individuals that constitute the State and grant power to the State to function on their behalf.[10] It "serves to divide between nations the space upon which human activities are employed, in order to assume them at all points the minimum of protection of which international law is the guardian."[11]

In international law, sovereignty is a legal concept with legal implications, unlike its understanding in political science.[12] This was systematically articulated in the famous *Island of Palmas* case in the following words:

> The fact that the functions of a State can be performed by any State within a given zone is on the other hand, precisely the characteristic feature of the *legal situation* pertaining in those parts of the globe which, like the high seas or lands without a master, cannot or do not yet form the territory of a State.[13] [emphasis added]

Also, as noted by Brownlie, sovereignty represents "the legal competence which States have in general, to refer to a particular function of this competence, or to provide a rationale for a particular aspect of the competence."[14]

Several inherent rights flow from the possession of sovereignty. The competences sovereignty entails are multiple and they are flexibly determined. The Declaration on Friendly Relations between States acknowledged this position in the following words:

10 Luzius Wildhaber, "Sovereignty and International Law" in *The Structure and Process of International Law: Essays in Legal Philosophy, Doctrine, and Theory*, ed. R. St. J. Macdonald, Douglas M. Johnston (The Hague: Kluwer Boston, 1983), 438.

11 *Island of Palmas case (Netherlands, USA)*, (1928) 2 RIAA 829 (4 April 1928), 839.

12 Marek Korowicz, "Some Present Aspects of Sovereignty in International Law" *Recueil des Cours* 102 (1961): 5, 14–16; see Ian Brownlie, "The Reality and Efficacy of International Law" *British Yearbook of International Law* 52, no. 1 (1981).

13 *Island of Palmas case (Netherlands, USA)*, (1928) 2 RIAA 829 (4 April 1928), 838.

14 Ian Brownlie, *Principles of Public International Law* (7th ed., Oxford: Oxford University Press, 2008), 291.

> Each State enjoys *the rights inherent* in *full sovereignty*.[15] [emphasis added]

The contents of the Declaration have been declared customary international law by the International Court of Justice ('ICJ') on more than one occasion.[16] The 'competences' and 'rights' are multiple, varied and cannot be identified exhaustively. The rights and competences are a manifestation of the underlying authority which a State possesses due to its character as a State and repository of public interest and the collective will of its constituents. Sovereignty is therefore a legal concept with multiple aspects. Accordingly, sovereignty is described as a "bundle of rights".[17]

Sovereignty has external and internal aspects. External aspects represent the power of the State to engage in international relations, whereas internal aspects represent the power to regulate affairs within its territories.[18] There is a negative as well as positive aspect of sovereignty. The negative aspect represents the authority to exclude interference of others whereas its positive aspect represents the enabling authority to regulate affairs within its territory.[19] Regulatory freedom is a positive enabling power emanating from sovereignty and an aspect of the internal sovereignty and the authority to resist external interferences in the State's internal administration.

Regulatory freedom is the prominent attribute of sovereignty which gives States the plenary power to regulate its internal affairs.[20] State is an institution which possess the monopoly to regulate the internal affairs.[21] Therefore the

---

15 UN General Assembly, Declaration on Principles of International Law concerning Friendly Relations and Co-operation among States in accordance with the Charter of the United Nations, A/RES/2625(XXV) 24 October 1970.

16 *Military and Paramilitary Activities in and against Nicaragua (Nicaragua v United States of America)*, [1986] ICJ Reports 14 (27 June 1986), para. 187; *Armed Activities on the Territory of the Congo (Democratic Republic of the Congo v Uganda)*, Judgment, [2005] ICJ Reports 168 (19 December 2005), para. 162.

17 Comments by David Kennedy, "How should sovereignty be defended?" *Politics Without Sovereignty: A Critique of Contemporary International Relations*, ed. Christopher Bickerton and others (Routledge, 2006). pp. 187–188.

18 Luzius Wildhaber, "Sovereignty and International Law" in *The Structure and Process of International Law: Essays in Legal Philosophy, Doctrine, and Theory*, ed. R. St. J. Macdonald, Douglas M. Johnston (The Hague: Kluwer Boston, 1983), 435–436.

19 *Island of Palmas case (Netherlands, USA)*, (1928) 2 RIAA 829, (4 April 1928) 839.

20 *Military and Paramilitary Activities in and against Nicaragua (Nicaragua v United States of America)*, [1986] ICJ Reports 14, 133 (27 June 1986); Samantha Besson, "Sovereignty" in *Max Planck Encyclopedia of Public International Law*, ed. Rüdiger Wolfrum (New York: Oxford University Press, 2008), paras. 120–121.

21 Martin Laughlin, *The Idea of Public Law* (Oxford: Oxford University Press, 2004), 84.

power to make laws is an important manifestation of sovereignty.[22] According to the Permanent Court of International Justice ('PCIJ'), "legislation is one of the most obvious forms of the exercise of sovereign power."[23] The power to make regulations flows from sovereignty. The authority to change the legal framework is an integral part of sovereignty; Oakeshott treats it as the characteristic of sovereignty. In his words: "the authority and the procedures to emancipate itself continuously from its legal past", in the sense that "there was no law so ancient and so entrenched that it could not be amended or repealed."[24]

Also, sovereignty is an "evolutionary concept" comprising of flexibility to address different situations arising in different times.[25] Sovereignty is flexible and divisible.[26] Sovereignty encompasses the general plenary power of the State to address different circumstances arising from time to time. These occurrences cannot be fixed in time or to specific situations. Regulatory freedom as a part of sovereignty plays a crucial role when it comes to economic activities. As a part of exercise of sovereignty, economic activities are conducted within States which gives the power to States to regulate economic activities in light of broader public interest goals.[27]

Regulatory freedom emanates from State sovereignty, which in turn in positive international law is a legal concept. Sovereignty is omnipresent linked to the very character of a State and so is regulatory freedom as its prominent component. States need not mention it in each legal instrument such as a treaty to claim it and exercise rights under it. Judge Weiss articulated this position in his opinion in the *Lotus* case in the following words:

22 J Brierly, *The Law of Nations* (5th ed., Oxford: Clarendon Press, 1955), 7.

23 *Legal Status of Eastern Greenland* (1933) PCIJ Series No. 53 (5 April 1933), 48.

24 Michael Oakeshott, "On the Chartacter of a Modern European State" in *On Human Conduct*, ed. Michael Oakeshott (Oxford: Clarendon Press, 1975), 182–326.

25 Kal Raustiala, "Rethinking the Sovereignty Debate in International Economic Law" *Journal of International Economic Law* 6 (2003): 841, 860–862; José Alvarez, "State Sovereignty Is Not Withering Away: A Few Lessons for the Future" in *Realizing Utopia: The Future of International Law*, ed. Antonio Cassese (Oxford: Oxford University Press, 2012), 31.

26 *United States – Measures Affecting the Cross Border Supply of Gambling and Betting Services*, WT DS 285/R (10 November 2004), para. 124.

27 Asif Qureshi, "Sovereignty Issues in the WTO Dispute Settlement – A "Development Sovereignty" Perspective" in *Redefining Sovereignty in International Economic Law*, ed. Wenhua Shan, Penelope Simons and Dalvinder Singh (USA: Hart Publishing, 2008), 162; Comments by Michael W Doyle, "How should sovereignty be defended?" *Politics Without Sovereignty: A Critique of Contemporary International Relations*, ed. Christopher Bickerton and others (Routledge, 2006). pp. 191–192.

> Among the foremost of these rules there is one which is paramount and which does not even require to be embodied in a treaty: that is the rule sanctioning the sovereignty of States. It is never fully relinquished by entering into treaties. It continues to operate because it "characterizes powers and privileges resting on customary international law and independent of the particular consent of another state.[28]
>
> If States were not sovereign, no international law would be possible, since the purpose of this law precisely is to harmonize and reconcile the different sovereignties over which it exercises its sway."[29]

It is due to the multifaceted nature of sovereignty that States can restrict some aspects of sovereignty through a treaty. It would be a difficult proposition to sustain that States entirely lose sovereignty by entering into treaties. In any event, such a proposition was rejected in the first case decided by the PCIJ – the *Wimbledon* case where the PCIJ treated the act of entering into treaties as exercise of sovereignty and the authority of the State to bind itself by parting some aspects of that sovereignty.[30] While the decision of the court was carried with a single vote, the dissenting and separate opinions have not expressed any objection to the observations of the majority of the Court on the role of sovereignty and limits on it cannot be implied. Even if some aspects are given away through a treaty other remain in the residue due to the multifaceted nature of sovereignty.[31] In the absence of specific exclusion, regulatory freedom is saved by the permissible rule whereby restrictions on exercise of sovereign rights cannot be presumed until expressly stated.[32] Few tribunals have advanced the position that regulatory freedom will not be available unless it is expressly mentioned and so secured in the treaty. These are discussed below.

---

28 Ian Brownlie, *Principles of Public International Law* (7th ed., Oxford: Oxford University Press, 2008), 291.

29 *The Case of the S.S. 'Lotus' (France v Turkey)*, (Dissenting Opinion of Judge Weiss), (1927) PCIJ Series A, No. 10 (7 September 1927), 4, 121.

30 *SS Wimbledon (Britain v Germany)*, Judgment, (1923) PCIJ Series A, No. 1 (17 August 1923), 25.

31 *Customs Régime Between German and Austria*, Advisory Opinion, PCIJ Series A/B, No. 41, (5 September 1931) 52; *Light Houses in Crete and Samos (France v Greece)*, Judgment, PCIJ Series A/B, No. 71 (8 October 1937), 103–104; Robert Jennings and Arthur Watts, ed., *Oppenheim's International Law*, vol. 1, 9th ed. (Harlow: Longman Group, 1992), 124–125.

32 For further analysis see Aniruddha Rajput, *Regulatory Freedom and Indirect Expropriation in Investment Arbitration* (Kluwer International, 2018), pp. 111–121; *The Case of the S.S. 'Lotus' (France v Turkey)*, (Dissenting Opinion of Judge Weiss), (1927) PCIJ Series A, No. 10 (7 September 1927), 19.

It seems that tribunals have disallowed regulatory freedom in light of treaty obligations due the possibility of unlimited discretion being left for the States, which may be used to defeat treaty obligations. Hence these tribunals have entirely disallow regulatory freedom. In *ADC v Hungary*, the tribunal began by acknowledging that "a sovereign State possesses the inherent right to regulate its domestic affairs" but this right "is not unlimited and must have its boundaries."[33] These boundaries however, according to the tribunal, were a result of "the rule of law, which includes treaty obligations".[34] As a result of this reasoning an IIA is a part of rule of law and a regulatory measure would constitute a violation of the rule of law and consequentially of the IIA. Rejecting the possibility of any scope for regulatory freedom due to the presence of an IIA, the tribunal concluded:

> Therefore, when a State enters into a bilateral investment treaty like the one in this case, it becomes bound by it and the investment- protection obligations it undertook therein must be honoured rather than be ignored by a later argument of the State's right to regulate.[35]

For the tribunal in *Achemia v Slovak Republic*, States are free to choose policies and an investment treaty is not "hostile towards particular policies". The focus of the treaty is only on "the manner in which policies may be changed and implemented, not on the policies themselves." The manner of adoption, as per the tribunal, meant in compliance with the investment treaty and no public policy can be justified for its violation.[36] A rather intriguing observation of the tribunal was

> Indeed, the Contracting Parties could go further, and exclude health care altogether from the coverage of the BIT if they so wish. But as long as the provisions of the Treaty remain in force and applicable, they must be respected. That is what the Governments of the Contracting Party

33 *ADC Affiliate Limited and ADC & ADMC Management Limited v. Republic of Hungary*, ICSID Case No. ARB/03/16, Award (2 October 2006), para. 423.

34 *ADC Affiliate Limited and ADC & ADMC Management Limited v. Republic of Hungary*, ICSID Case No. ARB/03/16, Award (2 October 2006), para. 423.

35 *ADC Affiliate Limited and ADC & ADMC Management Limited v. Republic of Hungary*, ICSID Case No. ARB/03/16, Award (2 October 2006), para. 423.

36 *Achmea B.V. (formerly Eureko B.V.) v. Slovak Republic I*, PCA Case No. 2008-13, Final Award (7 December 2012), para. 294.

> intended when they chose to conclude the Treaty, for what they judged to be the benefit of their States and their nationals.[37]

It is impossible and impractical to imagine a treaty to provide a comprehensive list of regulations excluded from the effect of an investment treaty.

However, sovereignty in international law is not "absolute, unlimited, arbitrary, [and] totalitarian"; it is the one "founded on a constituted legal order of checks and balances."[38] It represents "the final and determining power according to the existing legal order … means the highest legislative power and as such the 'constituted' power of the state community." While political sovereignty is "unfettered and absolute", "legal sovereignty is legally bound" and, in that sense "merely relative."[39] The constraints on sovereignty arise out of its elements as understood in customary international law. The discussion in Chapter VI below elaborates the contents of regulatory freedom which must be established to claim that a measure falls under regulatory freedom under international law.

Each of the aspects of sovereignty possess different normative value. Most of the aspects of sovereignty are customary international law, but some of them, such as the prohibition of acquisition of territory of another State by breaching territorial integrity and the right of self-determination are *jus cogens*.[40] Arguably at the conceptual level, being derived from sovereignty they possess

---

37 *Achmea B.V. (formerly Eureko B.V.) v. Slovak Republic I*, PCA Case No. 2008-13, Final Award (7 December 2012), para. 294; also see *Sergei Paushok, CJSC Golden East Company and CJSC Vostokneftegaz Company v. The Government of Mongolia*, UNCITRAL, Award on Jurisdiction and Liability (28 April 2011), para. 298; *Bear Creek Mining Corporation v. Republic of Peru*, ICSID Case No. ARB/14/21, Award (30 November 2017), para. 473.

38 Luzius Wildhaber, "Sovereignty and International Law" in *The Structure and Process of International Law: Essays in Legal Philosophy, Doctrine, and Theory*, ed. R. St. J. Macdonald, Douglas M. Johnston (The Hague: Kluwer Boston, 1983), 429; E N Van Kleffens, "Sovereignty in International Law" *Recueil des Cours* 82 (1953): 5, 127–128.

39 Luzius Wildhaber, "Sovereignty and International Law" in *The Structure and Process of International Law: Essays in Legal Philosophy, Doctrine, and Theory*, ed. R. St. J. Macdonald, Douglas M. Johnston (The Hague: Kluwer Boston, 1983), 429. Also see *Reservations to the Convention on the Prevention and Punishment of the Crime of Genocide* (Advisory Opinion) (1951) ICJ Reports 15, 24 (28 May 1951).

40 Samantha Besson, "Sovereignty" in *Max Planck Encyclopedia of Public International Law*, ed. Rüdiger Wolfrum (New York: Oxford University Press, 2008), para. 89; Luzius Wildhaber, "Sovereignty and International Law" in *The Structure and Process of International Law: Essays in Legal Philosophy, Doctrine, and Theory*, ed. R. St. J. Macdonald, Douglas M. Johnston (The Hague: Kluwer Boston, 1983), 424–444; James Crawford, *The Creation of States in International Law* (2nd ed., Oxford: Oxford University Press, 2006), 107.

the legal character of customary international law. However, this by itself is not sufficient to conclude that regulator freedom is customary international law. It is necessary that regulatory freedom satisfies the requirements laid down in international law to decide if a certain principle has attained the status of customary international law. The following chapter seeks to establish that there is enough evidence to establish that regulatory freedom satisfies the formal requirements to establish that it is a rule of customary international law.

2 Evidence of Regulatory Freedom as a Rule of Customary International Law

Custom is a "clear and continuous habit of doing certain actions which has grown up under the aegis of the conviction that these actions are, according to international law, obligatory or right."[41] Article 38 (1) (b) defines custom "as evidence of a general practice accepted as law." This phrase, along with the progression of jurisprudence on the point has resulted to the development of the twin requirements to establish a rule of customary international law: State practice and *opinio juris*.[42]

The evidence of State practice may be found in various physical and verbal acts of a State.[43] State practice may take the form of "diplomatic acts and correspondence; conduct in connection with resolutions adopted b an international organization or at an intergovernmental conference; conduct in connection with treaties; executive conduct, including operational conduct "on the ground"; legislative and administrative acts; and decisions of national courts."[44] While assessing practice, to decide if there is sufficient State practice to establish a custom, the entire practice of States is to be seen as a whole. The weight given to the practice depends on the circumstances.[45] The generality of practice does not require absolute and perfect presence of practice otherwise

41 Robert Jennings and Arthur Watts, ed., *Oppenheim's International Law*, vol. 1, 9th ed. (Harlow: Longman Group, 1992), 27.

42 International Law Commission, Conclusion 2, Identification of Customary International Law, A/73/10 (2018), 117; Ian Brownlie, *Principles of Public International Law* (7th ed., Oxford: Oxford University Press, 2008), 6–7.

43 International Law Commission, Conclusion 6, Identification of Customary International Law, A/73/10 (2018), 117.

44 International Law Commission, Conclusion 6(2), Identification of Customary International Law, A/73/10 (2018), 117.

45 International Law Commission, Conclusion 7, Identification of Customary International Law, A/73/10 (2018), 117.

establishing a custom will be impossible.[46] It is sufficient if the practice is sufficiently widespread and representative.[47]

Equally, the State practice is to be accompanied with the psychological belief of the existence of a legal obligation that required or accompanied State practice. Meaning that the actions taken or restraint from acting were undertaken with a sense of a binding obligation – expressed in the phrase *opinio juris siv necessiatis*.[48] The evidence of *opinio juris* may take a wide range of forms.[49] These may include but are not limited to "public statements made on behalf of States; official publications; government legal opinions; diplomatic correspondence; decisions of national courts; treaty provisions; and conduct in connection with resolutions adopted by an international organization or at an intergovernmental conference."[50]

The following six categories of evidence establish that regulatory freedom satisfies both State practice and *opinio juris*.

First, the practice of organs of a State, especially executive is a good evidence of practice.[51] Especially, statements of government officials are an important evidence of State practice and *opinio juris*.[52] In the statements of government officials, regulatory freedom – that is the freedom to undertake regulations and not having to compensate for consequential financial losses – has been asserted. After the British Parliament introduced wide ministerial powers allowing introduction of approvals, conduct of price and modifications of terms of contract, including retrospective alterations through the Petroleum and Sub Pipelines Act of 1975, oil companies objected to the possibility of exercise of wide regulatory freedom. In response, the Secretary of Energy in the United Kingdom took the following position:

---

46 *Military and Paramilitary Activities in and against Nicaragua* (*Nicaragua v United States of America*), [1986] ICJ Reports 14 (27 June 1986), para. 186.

47 International Law Commission, Conclusion 8, Identification of Customary International Law, A/73/10 (2018), 117.

48 International Law Commission, Conclusion 9, Identification of Customary International Law, A/73/10 (2018), 117.

49 International Law Commission, Conclusion 10, Identification of Customary International Law, A/73/10 (2018), 117.

50 International Law Commission, Conclusion 10(2), Identification of Customary International Law, A/73/10 (2018), 117.

51 Yoram Dinstein, "The Interaction Between Customary International Law and Treaties" *Recueil des Cours* 322 (2006): 259, 269–270.

52 Yoram Dinstein, "The Interaction Between Customary International Law and Treaties" *Recueil des Cours* 322 (2006): 259, 275–281.

> The change in the legal framework that is available to governments and is regularly used by a whole host of environmental, health, tax, and other measures, does not include the provision to compensation as a result.[53]

Furthermore, making a distinction between regulatory measure and an expropriatory measure, the Secretary of State asserted that there was no responsibility to compensate for a regulatory measure since the losses arising out of such measures do not constitute expropriation. The alterations of regulatory framework may involve "new taxation, exchange control, safety or other requirements also modify government profits but it is everywhere accepted that these measures do not necessitate the payment of compensation."[54] The same position was taken by the Canadian government to justify similar measures.[55]

The absence of objection from other States to these statements when they were expected to react (protest) shows their acquiescence to this practice.[56] In this specific instance, it would be reasonable to expect objections from other States, especially from the States where these oil companies originated from. But no objections were raised by other States. Especially considering that the oil companies faced financial losses as a result of regulatory exercises and none of the other States took up that cause or objected to the UK and Canadian position. The context within which these assertions were made and the silence or absence of protest from other States is sufficiently supportive to conclude the presence of regulatory freedom as a rule of customary law. The practice of these States is particularly important since there are specially affected States. They have traditionally been capital exporting States and have given precedence to rights of investor protection at the time when they indulged in this practice. Also, this is a specific and precise practice on regulatory freedom without the responsibility to compensate for the losses caused due to regulatory freedom.[57]

---

53 Hansard, House of Commons Standing Committee D (3 July 1975), cols. 1146–1172.

54 Hansard, House of Commons Standing Committee D (28 July 1975), cols. 1439–1440.

55 See EMendes, "The Canadian National Energy Programme: An Example of Assertion of Sovereignty or Creeping Expropriation in International Law" *Vanderbilt Journal of Transnational Law* 14 (1981): 475, 480.

56 Michael Akehurst, "Custom as a Source of International Law" *British Yearbook of International Law* 47, no. 1 (1975): 38; International Law Commission, Conclusion 2, Identification of Customary International Law, A/73/10 (2018), 117.

57 Michael Akehurst, "Custom as a Source of International Law" *British Yearbook of International Law* 47, no. 1 (1975): 21; International Law Commission, Conclusion 7, Identification of Customary International Law, A/73/10 (2018), 117.

The Third American Restatement of Foreign Relations Law of the United States is of particular relevance since it specifies international law obligations and rights of the United States. It acknowledges regulatory freedom in the following words:

> A state is not responsible for loss of property or for other economic disadvantages resulting from bona fide general taxation, regulation, forfeiture for crime, or other action of the kind that is commonly accepted as within the police power of states, if it is not discriminatory. [...] and is not designed to cause the alien to abandon the property to the state or sell it at a distress price.[58]

More prominently the General Assembly resolutions on permanent sovereignty over natural resources[59] and the Charter of Economic Rights and Duties of States[60] are based on and contain same expression of the legal principle.

Third, the treaty practice of States,[61] including through the Model BITs[62] which are a representation of State's policy towards foreign investment has evolved in a manner to show the insistence upon the exercise of regulatory

58 *Restatement of the Law Third, The Foreign Relations Law of the United States* (American Law Institute, 1987), 201.

59 UN General Assembly, Permanent Sovereignty over Natural Resources, G.A.res.1803(XVII), 17 U.N.GAOR Supp. (No. 17) at 15, U.N. Doc. A/5217 (1962), (Foreign investment agreements freely entered into by or between sovereign States shall be observed in good faith; States and international organizations shall strictly and conscientiously respect the sovereignty of peoples and nations over their natural wealth and resources in accordance with the Charter and the principles set forth in the present resolution).

60 UN General Assembly, Charter of Economic Rights and Duties of States, G.A. res. 3281 (XXIX), 12 December 1974, arts. 6, 7, 9, 16, chap. III.

61 Comprehensive Economic Cooperation Agreement between The Republic of India and the Republic of Singapore, 2005, https://commerce.gov.in/international-trade/trade-agreements/comprehensive-economic-cooperation-agreement-between-the-republic-of-india-and-the-republic-of-singapore/.; United States – Singapore Free Trade Agreement, 2004, art. 9.4, https://ustr.gov/trade-agreements/free-trade-agreements/singapore-fta/final-text.

62 Treaty Between the Government of the United States of America and the Government of [country] concerning the encouragement an reciprocal protection of investment, 2012, https://ustr.gov/sites/default/files/BIT%20text%20for%20ACIEP%20Meeting.pdf; Model Agreement Between Canada and [...] for the Promotion and Protection of Investments (2021), Government of Canada, 12 May 2021, https://www.international.gc.ca/trade-commerce/trade-agreements-accords-commerciaux/agr-acc/fipa-apie/2021_model_fipa-2021_modele_apie.aspx?lang=eng; Investmet Cooperation and Facilitation Treaty between The Federative Republic of Brazil and The Republic of India, 25 January 2020, accessed June 29 2024, art. 4, https://dea.gov.in/sites/default/files/Investment%20

freedom. The activity of increasing number of States in this regard shows the practice and *opinio juris*.[63]

Fourth, pleadings by States before international courts and tribunals constitute evidence of State practice and *opinio juris*. These pleadings are important from two perspectives: they serve to confirm custom and also contribute towards its creation.[64] States have asserted the presence of regulatory freedom as a rule of customary international law in their pleadings before various international courts and tribunals. In the *ELSI* case both Italy and the US asserted regulatory freedom. Italy referred to regulatory freedom as 'police regulations'[65] and argued that regulatory freedom cannot be ignored simply because the State has entered into a treaty regulating the subject matter of the over which regulatory freedom is exercised.[66] The US argued that when States enter into treaty relations and undertake obligations, they are mindful that the prerogative powers of the State are not eliminated or dramatically reduced.[67] Even where a State has objected to the exercise of regulatory freedom, the objection is not aimed at the presence of the right to regulate but to whether the losses caused due to the challenged actions fall within the purview of regulatory freedom. The challenge to substantive exercise of regulatory freedom is based purely on the question of whether that exercise fall within the authorization to exercise regulatory freedom under domestic law.[68]

Cooperation%20and%20Facilitation%20Treaty%20with%20Brazil%20-%20English_0.pdf.

63 Michael Akehurst, "Custom as a Source of International Law" *British Yearbook of International Law* 47, no. 1 (1975): 19; International Law Commission, Conclusion 11(1)(c), Identification of Customary International Law, A/73/10 (2018), 117.

64 *Mexican Railway Union Claim*, where the reply by the State was considered as the sole evidence of the rule in question, 1930 RIAA vol. 5, 115 (10 February 1930), 122–4.; *Eschauzier claim* (1931) RIAA 207 (24 June 1931), 210–2; *Mergé Claim* (1955) ILR 22 443 (10 June 1955), 449–50; *re Piracy Jure Gentium* [1934] AC 586, 599–600; Michael Akehurst, "Custom as a Source of International Law" *British Yearbook of International Law* 47, no. 1 (1975): 4–5.

65 International Court of Justice, Reports of Judgments, Advisory Opinions and Orders, *Case concerning Elettronica Sicula S.p.A. (ELSI) (United States of America v. Italy)*, Judgment of 20 July 1989; Rejoinder of Italy in ELSI, Doc. 13096, (20 July 1989), p. 460.

66 International Court of Justice, Pleadings, Oral Arguments, Documents, *Case concerning Elettronica Sicula S.p.A. (ELSI) (United States of America v. Italy)*, Vol. II: Counter-Memorial; Reply; Rejoinder, p. 35.

67 International Court of Justice, Pleadings, Oral Arguments, Documents, *Case concerning Elettronica Sicula S.p.A. (ELSI) (United States of America v. Italy)*, Annex to Memorial of United States, p. 396.

68 International Court of Justice, Pleadings, Oral Arguments, Documents, *Case concerning Elettronica Sicula S.p.A. (ELSI) (United States of America v. Italy)*, Pleadings of United States, p. 382–3.

Regulatory freedom is not unique on matters relating to investor protection. The right to exercise regulatory freedom as a part of customary international law has been raised by States and upheld by international courts and tribunals in other areas of international law as well. In the *Navigation Rights* Case, both the parties Nicaragua and Costa Rica agreed on the presence of regulatory freedom. The disagreement was limited to the scope of activities covered within that regulatory freedom.[69] Regulatory freedom was, as argued by Costa Rica, emerged from sovereignty.[70]

Regulatory freedom has been asserted by several States in proceedings before the World Trade Organization (WTO).[71] United States defended its measures for environment protection in the following way:

> The United States responds that Article XX (b) and (g) contain no jurisdictional limitations, not limitations on the location of the animals or natural resources to be protected and conserved and that, under general principles of international law relating to sovereignty, States have the right to regulate imports within their jurisdiction.[72]

Equally, Australia defended regulatory freedom in the following words:

> Australia further stated that the Panel was not being asked to determine whether contracting parties had the right to enforce unilaterally-determined standards. In circumstances where unilateral standards were not enforced by trade or trade-related measures, there was obviously

69 International Court of Justice, Reports of Judgments, Advisory Opinions and Orders, *Dispute regarding Navigational and Related Rights* (*Costa Rica v. Nicaragua*), Memorial of Costa Rica, para.4.03; Nicaragua, Acting Foreign Minister Carlos Gurdián, Note to Costa Rican Foreign Minister Roberto Rojas López, Note No. MRE/98/02638, 28 August 1998, Annexes, Vol. 3, Annex 51.

70 International Court of Justice, Reports of Judgments, Advisory Opinions and Orders, *Dispute regarding Navigational and Related Rights* (*Costa Rica v. Nicaragua*), Memorial of Costa Rica, Pleadings, para.5.89 citing Nicaraguan Foreign Minister Norman Caldera Cardenal to Costa Rican Foreign Minister Roberto Tovar Faja, Note No. MRWDM-3111284/11/05, 9 November 2005, Annexes, Vol. 3, Annex 82.

71 *United States – Measures Affecting the Cross-Border Supply of Gambling and Betting Services*, Report of the Panel, WT/DS285 (10 November 2004), para.5.1.6; *China–Measures Affecting Trading Rights and Distribution Services for Certain Publications and Audiovisual Entertainment Products*, Report of the Appellate Body, WT/DS363/AB/R (21 December 2009), para. 46..

72 *United States – Import Prohibition of Certain Shrimp and Shrimp Products*, Report of the Panel, WT/DS58, (15 May 1998), para. 7.24.

> no role for the GATT. In most instances, it was possible to enforce such standards without risk to GATT obligations, including GATT rules of non-discrimination. In other instances, GATT exceptions provisions might be invoked in line with sovereignty principles. The text of the General Agreement clearly respected the sovereign right of contracting parties to maintain their own standards. However, sovereignty was a two-way street in the GATT. A contracting party which claimed the right to take trade restrictions based on unilaterally-determined standards must expect other contracting parties to claim the right to justify trade restrictions against that contracting party on the same grounds. The United States intermediary nation embargo effectively denied other contracting parties subject to the embargo the sovereignty to set their own standards for the like product.[73]

Pleadings of States in investment arbitration cases provide ample support for regulatory freedom as a rule of customary international law. The pleading of Canada in *Chemtura v Canada* systematically and comprehensively presented the basis of regulatory freedom in customary international law with a reference to all precedents and practice.[74]

Fifth, custom is also reflected in the internal behavior of States.[75] National legislations are an important evidence to establish custom. States rely on laws of various States to establish practice and the ICJ has recognized the role of national legislations as evidence of customary international law.[76] Several constitutions and other legislative provisions permit States to undertake regulations in public interest without the responsibility to compensate for losses caused to private parties.[77]

Sixth, decisions of international courts and tribunals are subsidiary sources of international law but they may contain evidence of customary international

73 *United States–Restrictions on Imports of Tuna*, Report of the Panel, DS29/R (16 June 1994), para.4.2.

74 *Crompton (Chemtura) Corp. v. Government of Canada*, PCA Case No. 2008-01, Respondent's Counter-Memorial, UNCITRAL (20 October 2008), paras. 565–594.

75 Robert Jennings and Arthur Watts, ed., *Oppenheim's International Law*, vol. 1, 9th ed. (Harlow: Longman Group, 1992), 26.

76 *Nottebohm (Liechtenstein v Guatemala)*, Second Phase, Judgment, (1955) ICJ Reports 4 (6 April 1955), 22; *Panevezys- Saldutiskis Railway*, Judgment, PCIJ Series A/B, No. 76 (28 February 1939), 923.

77 Andrevander Walt, *Constitutional Property Clauses: A Comparative Analysis* (The Hague: Kluwer Law International, 1999), 19; for examples from constitutions of commonwealth countries see Tom Allen, *The Right to Property in Commonwealth Constitutions* (Cambridge: Cambridge University Press, 2000), 162.

law. Also, they carry great value due to the tendency to rely on them by later courts and tribunals. Extensive judicial practice spanning over a wide range of duration and across various areas of international law has recognized regulatory freedom and the ability of States to undertake regulations that affects rights of private persons without having to compensate for the consequential losses.[78] Exercise of regulatory freedom operates as an exception from responsibility for an internationally wrongful act.[79] Various national and regional courts have also recognized regulatory freedom in their decisions.[80] The Appellate Body of the WTO accepted that unless specifically given away regulatory freedom is unaffected.[81] Several investment tribunals have also confirmed that regulatory freedom is a rule of customary international law.[82]

The above discussion is sufficient to indicate that regulatory freedom, apart from conceptually drawing its claim for customary international law as a part of sovereignty, there is sufficient evidence in State practice and *jus cogens* to establish that regulatory freedom is a rule of customary international law.

---

78 *The Robert Wilson case* (1841), Moore, History and Digest of Arbitration, etc. (1898), vol. IV, p.3373; and the *Louis Chazen International Arbitral case* (1930) 6 RIAA 564 (8 October 1930); *J Parsons case*, 6 RIAA 165 (1925); *Nielsen American and British Claims Arbitrations, etc.* 1926, 587; *Fabar case* (*United States v Yugoslavia*), Settlement of Claims by Foreign Claims Settlement Commission, 10 RIAA 438 (1955), 23; *Brewer, Moller & Co. case* (*Germany v Venezuela*) 10 RIAA 423 (1903); *Kugele v Polish State*, 6 Ann. Dig. 69 (1931–32); *Dickson Car Wheel Co. case*, 4 RIAA 669 (July 1931) Op of Com 174,192–3.

79 *Allgemine Gold und Silbersceideanstalt v Customs and Excise Commissioner*, (1980) 2 WLR 555; (1980) 51 BY 305; AKU case ILR 23 (1956), 21; *Assets of Hungarian Company in Germany case* ILR 32, 565; *Re Dohnert Muller, Schmidt & Company*, 570 cited in Ian Brownlie, *Principles of Public International Law* (7th ed., Oxford: Oxford University Press, 2008), at footnotes 83–85, at p. 536.

80 For a summary of relevant decisions see Aniruddha Rajput, *Regulatory Freedom and Indirect Expropriation in Investment Arbitration* (Kluwer International, 2018), pp. 130–132.

81 *United States- Measures Affecting the Cross-Border Supply of Gambling and Betting Services*, Report of the Panel, WT/DS285 (10 November 2004), para.5.1.7.

82 *Marvin Roy Feldman Karpa v. United Mexican States*, ICSID Case No. ARB(AF)/99/1, para. 103; *Link-Trading Joint Stock Company v. Department for Customs Control of the Republic of Moldova*, UNCITRAL, para. 68; *Saluka Investments BV v. The Czech Republic*, PCA Case No. 2001-04, paras. 255, 260, 262; *Crompton (Chemtura) Corp. v. Government of Canada*, PCA Case No. 2008-01, UNCITRAL (20 October 2008), paras 121, 122; *El Paso Energy International Company v. Argentine Republic*, ICSID Case No. ARB/03/15, para. 240.

CHAPTER 3

Regulatory Freedom and Treatment Standards: Interaction of Norms

Having established the legal nature of regulatory freedom in international law: that is regulatory freedom is a rule of customary international law; this chapter investigates the relationship between regulatory freedom and treatment standards as legal norms originating in two different sources – customs and treaties respectively. The relationship between regulatory freedom and treatment standards is explored based on the relationship between customary international law and treaty law; concurrent application of customary international law alongside treaty provisions and no presumed exclusion of customary international law; conflict of norms and jurisprudence of international courts and tribunals on the relationship between regulatory freedom and treaty obligations. This discussion is essential in order to determine whether regulatory freedom can be exercised despite the presence of obligations in the form of treatment standards in investment treaties.

1 Relationship between Customary International Law and Treaty Law

The manner in which regulatory freedom interacts with treatment standards and the extent to which the latter restricts or modifies former is governed by the principles regulating the relationship between custom and treaty as sources of international law. Precisely because regulatory freedom is a rule of customary international law and treatment standards emanate from treaty law.

The famous Article 38 (1), stipulates treaties and customs as sources of international law in the following words:

1. The Court, whose function is to decide in accordance with international law such disputes as are submitted to it, shall apply:
   a. international conventions, whether general or particular, establishing rules expressly recognized by the contesting states;
   b. international custom, as evidence of a general practice accepted as law;

The presentation of treaties and custom in a certain order may give the impression that treaties are to be preferred over custom. An extreme approach on the end of that spectrum would be absolute superiority of treaties over custom

 | DOI:10.1163/9789004759831_004

leaving little or no room for customary international law. In practical terms, it is easy to apply treaties first because normally, the norms contained in treaties can be easily identified and applied, unlike customary international law rules that require a complex process to identify them, as was already discussed above in Chapter II above. Therefore, it is natural for an adjudicator to first apply a treaty before moving to any other source.

Whether this practical convenience of treaties made them superior to custom was a matter discussed by the Committee of Jurists during the drafting of what became Article 38 (1). A proposal was made that the sources shall be applied in succession – *en ordre successif* – that is first a treaty would be applied and only if a treaty was absent then the adjudicator would move to custom and other sources. This proposal was rejected. The manner of presentation of treaties and custom in Article 38 (1) only means that there is a sequence of application but no priority *per se*.[1] Treaties and customs have an "equal relationship of interdependence and mutual support."[2] They are equally binding.[3] Both treaties and customs are expressions of State consent: in the former, the consent is express and in the latter, it is implied.[4] Applying these principles to the present context, it is beyond doubt that there is no precedence in favour of treatment standards over regulatory freedom. Regulatory freedom and treatment standards are of the same normative value and are to be simultaneously applied.

Contrary to the impression that a treaty ought to have precedence over custom, the nature of the norms contained in a treaty, as opposed to custom is such that customary international law cannot be lightly taken or ignored. A treaty is a contractual arrangement where obligations are identified and taken bilaterally or multilaterally. This has led scholars to argue that treaties do not create international law as such because they apply within the limited rubric

1 For a detailed discussion on the issue of hierarchy and the discussions from the drafting history see Michael Akehurst, "The Hierarchy of the Sources of International Law" *British Yearbook of International Law* 47, no. 1 (1975): 274, 274–277.

2 L. Condorelli, "Customary International Law: The Yesterday, Today, and Tomorrow of General International Law" in *Realizing Utopia: The Future of International Law*, ed. Antonio Cassese (Oxford University Press, 2012), 149–50.

3 Mark Villiger, *Customary International Law and Treaties: A Manual on the Theory and Practice of the Interrelation of Sources* (The Hague: Kluwer Law International, 1997), 58–59.

4 Georg Shwarzenberger, *International Law as applied by International Court and Tribunals* (London, Stevans and Sons Ltd. 1945); VD Degan, *Sources of International Law* (The Netherlands: Martinus Nijhoff Publishers, 1997), 181; D. Anzilotti, *Cours de droit international Public* (Paris: Libarairie de Recueil Sirey, 1929), 89–93; A Cavaligeri, *Corso di dirittointernazionale*, Tezaedizione, Napoli 1939, 63, K Struoo, "Les regales generals du droit le la paix" RCV 1934 tom 47, 14.

of the consent of the parties to the treaty.[5] Therefore the obligations contained in a treaty, by themselves do not have a normative value, unless those norms have on their own achieved the status of peremptory norms of international law (*jus cogens*), customary international law or general principles of law. In which case the treaty will be codifying existing legal norms. Thus, treatment standards get legal value because they are part of an IIA – that is a treaty. Unless they are a part of the codification process. Regulatory freedom on the other hand, being a rule of customary international law possesses a normative value independent of its reference or absence of any reference to it in a treaty. Customary international law is therefore, inevitably accorded prominence. It has universal application and at the general level it facilitates the coherence of the entire system of international law.[6] Therefore, the presence of an IIA and standards of treatment does not exclude the application of customary international law. Customary international law, that is regulatory freedom continues to apply concurrently with treatment standards.

The concurrent application of treaties and customs and the need of clear exclusion of customary international law through treaty law is discussed in the following section.

2 Concurrent Application and No Presumed Exclusion of Custom

International investment law, more or less – if not entirely, is a set of legal principles arising out of legal norms contained in IIAs. International investment law is a specialized regime to the extent that it contains rules that regulate relations between foreign investors and States. The characterisation of international investment law as a specialized regime is not sufficient to isolate ti from general international law and exclude the operation of customary international law. In fact, all specialized regimes, irrespective of the area of international law they cover, function within the framework of general international law. They

5 Gerald Fitzmaurice, "Some Problems Regarding the Formal Sources of International Law" in *Symbolae Verzijl: présentées au professeur J.H.W. Verzijl à l'occasion de son LXXième anniversaire*, ed. J.H.W. Vezjil (The Hague: Martinus Nijhodd; 1958), 157–58. Also republished in Martti Koskenniemi, *Sources of International Law* (England: Ashgate, 2000).

6 Oscar Schachter, "Entangled Treaty and Custom" in *International Law at a Time of Perplexity: Essays in Honour of Shabtai Rosenne*, ed. Yoram Distein & Mala Tabory (Dordrecht, Boston, London: Martinus Nijhoff Publishers, 1989), 721; Luigi Condorelli, "Customary International Law: The Yesterday, Today, and Tomorrow of General International Law" in *Realizing Utopia: The Future of International Law*, ed. Antonio Cassese, (Oxford: Oxford University Press, 2012), 150.

cannot operate in isolation.[7] This is equally true for international investment law.[8] Even the ICJ has noted that the so-called specialised regime of international investment law does not exclude the application of general international law.[9]

Practically, it is impossible for a treaty to operate to the exclusion of or in the absence of customary international law. A treaty does not and cannot comprehensively govern all rights and obligations of the parties to a treaty, it has to rely on customary international law. The example of the WTO is noteworthy in this regard. The plain reading of the text of Article 3.2 of the Dispute Settlement Understanding ('DSU') of the WTO indicates that the only role of customary international law in relation to the WTO agreements is for treaty interpretation. But realizing the impracticality of such a narrow approach, Panels and Appellate Bodies have extensively relied on customary international law in areas other than treaty interpretation.[10] IIAs do not contain any provision that specifies a narrow funnel to apply customary international law like the WTO, therefore there are no reasons to exclude or narrow the application of customary international law. This position is acknowledged in the case law on investment arbitration as well.[11]

Moreover, a treaty is to be interpreted and applied with the awareness of the operation of other rules of international law, which are accommodated through the principle of systemic integration contained in Article 31 (3) (c) of the Vienna Convention on the Law of Treaties ('VCLT').[12] Article 31 (3) (c) requires that while interpreting a treaty in light of its object and purpose, "any relevant rules of international law applicable in the relations between the parties" has to be taken into account. The relevant rules of international law would be rules originating in all the sources of international

7 Bruno Simma and Dirk Pulkowski, "Of Planets and Universe: Self-contained Regimes in International Law", *European Journal of International Law* 17 (2006): 483, 492–493.

8 *Phoenix Action, Ltd. v The Czech Republic*, ICSID Case No. ARB/06/5, Award (15 April 2009), paras. 75–8.

9 *Case Concerning Ahmadou Sadio Diallo (Guinea v Congo)*, Preliminary Objections, Order, 46 ILM 712 (2007) (May 24 2007), para. 90.

10 For a detailed study on the topic see Joost Pauwelyn, *Conflict of Norms in Public International Law: How WTO Law Relates to Other Rules of International Law* (Cambridge: Cambridge University Press, 2003).

11 *Phoenix Action, Ltd. v The Czech Republic*, ICSID Case No. ARB/06/5, Award (15 April 2009), paras. 75–8.

12 Report of the Study Group of the International Law Commission, Fragmentation of International Law: Difficulties Arising From the Diversification and Expansion of International Law, A/CN.4/L.682 (2006), paras. 192–193.

law.[13] Prominently, as declared by the ICJ, relevant rules of general customary international law are a part of the applicable rules.[14] The approach of systemic integration has been upheld by international courts and tribunals.[15] Additionally, the rule of effective treaty interpretation requires that norms originating in different sources shall be interpreted in a manner that they both can stand and operate.[16] Consequentially, treatment standards as treaty rules and regulatory freedom as customary international law have to be interpreted and applied harmoniously.

Most importantly, the exclusion of customary international law rule by a treaty rule cannot be presumed. States are free to contract out of a specific rule of customary international law through a treaty but that exclusion has to be clearly established.[17] Exclusion of regulatory freedom – an element of

13 Campbell McLachlan, "The Principle of Systematic Integration and Article 31 (3) I of the Vienna Convention," *International and Comparative Law Quarterly* 54 (2005): 279, 361; TW Waelde, "Interpreting Investment Treaties: Experience and Examples" in *International Investment Law for the21st Century: Essays in Honour of Christoph Schreuer*, ed. Christina Binder, Ursula Kriebaum, August Reinisch & Stephan Wittich (Oxford: Oxford University Press, 2009); A Gourgourinis, "Lex Specialis in WTO and Investment Protection Law," *German Yearbook of International Law* 53 (2010): 579; A Gourgourinis, "The Distinction between Interpretation and Application of Norms in International Adjudication," *Journal of International Dispute Settlement* 2 (2011): 31; Alain Pellet, "The Case Law of the ICJ in Investment Arbitration," *International Centre for Settlement of Investment Disputes Review* 28 (2013): 223.

14 *Oil Platforms case (Iran v United States of America)*, Merits, Judgment, [2003] ICJ Rep. 161 (6 November 2003), para. 23, 41; *Asian Agricultural Products Ltd. (AAPL) v. Republic of Sri Lanka*, ICSID Case No. ARB/87/3, Award (27 June 1990), para. 41.

15 *Case Concerning Kasikili/Sedudu Islands (Bostwana v Namibia)*, Judgment, [1999] ICJ Rep. 1045 (13 December 1999), para. 93; *Oil Platforms case (Iran v United States of America)*, Merits, Judgment, [2003] ICJ Rep. 161 (6 November 2003), para. 41; also see (Separate opinion of Judge Simma), paras 5–16; (Separate opinion of Judge Higgins), paras 40–54; *United States- Standards for Reformulated and Conventional Gasoline*, WT/DS2/AB/R, DSR 1996: I, (20 May 1996) 16–17; *Korea – Measures Affecting Government Procurement*, WT/DS163, WT/DS163/R (19 January 2000), para. 7.96; *United States- Import Prohibition of Certain Shrimp and Shrimp Products*, WT/DS58/AB/R, DSR 1998:VII, Appellate Body, 2794–2797 (6 November 1998), paras 127–131; *Canada-Terms of Patent Protection*, Report of the Appellate Body, WT/DS170/AB/R (18 September 2000), paras 71–74; *Brazil – Export Financing Programme for Aircraft: Recourse to Arbitration by Brazil under Art. 22.6 of the DSU and Art. 4.11 of the SCM Agreement*, Decision by the Arbitrators, WT/DS46/ARB (28 August 2000), paras 3.6–3.10.

16 Alexander Orakhelashvili, *The Interpretation of Acts and Rules in Public International Law* (Oxford University Press, 2008), pp. 393–440.

17 *North Sea Continental Shelf Cases (Federal Republic of Germany/Denmark; Federal Republic of Germany/Netherlands)*, Judgment [1969] I.C.J. Reports 3 (20 February 1969) 42; *Case Concerning the Continental Shelf (Tunisia/Libyan Arab Jamahiriya)* Judgment, [1982] ICJ

sovereignty – has to be especially clear. Restrictions on sovereignty cannot be lightly presumed.[18] The act of entering into a treaty limits an element of sovereignty sought to be regulated by the treaty. Unless there is clear evidence of restrictions being undertaken in relation to a certain aspect of sovereignty, all other aspects of sovereignty, except the one being regulated continue to operate.[19] The principle *expression unius est exclusion alterius* represents the idea that nothing that is barred by the treaty is allowed.[20] Akehurst calls it "the presumption in favour of liberty of action".[21] The ICJ accentuated this point in the *ELSI case* in the following words:

> The Chamber has no doubt that the parties to a treaty can therein either agree that the local remedies rule shall not apply to claims based on alleged breaches of that treaty; or confirm that it shall apply. Yet the Chamber finds itself unable to accept that an important principle of customary international law should be held to have been tacitly dispensed with, in the absence of any words making clear an intention to do so.[22]

Likewise, in the *Chorzów Factory Case*, the PCIJ observed that:

> The silence of a treaty as to the existence of such a right cannot be interpreted as implying the exclusion of a right which has its source outside of the treaty, in general international law.[23]

Reports 18 (24 February 1982) 38; Joost Pauwelyn, *Conflict of Norms in Public International Law: How WTO Law Relates to Other Rules of International Law* (Cambridge: Cambridge University Press, 2003), 212–218.

18 *Free Zones of Upper Savoy and the District of Gex* (*France v Switzerland*) (1932) PCIJ Series A/B, No. 46, (19 August 1929) 167; Humphrey Waldock, "General Course on Public International Law" in *Collected Courses of The Hague Academy of International Law – Recueil des cours, Académie de Droit International de la Ha*, vol. 106 (1962), p. 418.

19 *The Case of The SS 'Wimbledon'* (*Britain v Germany*), Decision, (1923) PCIJ Series A, No. 1 (17 August 1923), 15, 25; *Customs Régime Between Germany and Australia*, Advisory Opinion, (1931) PCIJ Series A/B, No. 41 (5 September 1931), 37, 50–2.

20 *Case Concerning Certain German Interests in Polish Upper Silesia* (*Germany v Poland*), Judgment, (1925) PCIJ Series A-No. 7 (25 May 1926), 21–22.

21 Michael Akehurst, "Custom as a Source of International Law" *British Yearbook of International Law* 47, no. 1 (1975): 37.

22 *Elettronica Sicula S.P.A.* (*ELSI*) (*United States of America v Italy*), Judgment, [1989] ICJ Reports 15 (20 July 1989), 42.

23 *Legal Consequences for States of the Continued Presence of South Africa in Namibia* (*South West Africa*) *notwithstanding Security Council Resolution 276* (*1970*), Advisory Opinion, [1971] ICJ Reports 16 (21 June 1971), para. 96; *Free Zones of Upper Savoy and the District of Gex* [*France v Switzerland*] (1932) PCIJ Series A/B, No. 46 (19 August 1929), 167.

Regulatory freedom, that is a measure of a State that satisfies the elements of regulatory freedom as set out in customary international law is such an integral and important element of sovereignty that its exclusion cannot be presumed or lightly inferred. Its exclusion has to be clear and specific.[24] It is an error to think, as perceived in some scholarly writings that regulatory freedom is not available unless specifically preserved.[25] In the absence of a clear exclusion or limitations on regulatory freedom, regulatory freedom exists and States are free to exercise it.

True, regulatory freedom and treatment standards fall broadly under the same field of public international law: the relationship between foreign investors and States. Yet, the presence of treaty rules in the form of treatment standards is insufficient to exclude the operation of regulatory freedom. Rules of customary law continue to operate despite the presence of a treaty.[26] Even where a treaty deals comprehensively with rights of individuals other rules of customary international law continue to operate, as per the PCIJ in the *Jurisdiction of the Courts in Danzing* case.[27] Similarly, in the *La Grand* case and the *Tehran Hostage Crisis* case, the ICJ opined that the operation of the Vienna Convention on Diplomatic and Consular Relations did not exclude the operation of customary international law rules on diplomatic relations.[28] Taking a step further in the *Military and Paramilitary Activities* case, the ICJ declared that a treaty and a customary law rule may cover the same field and have identical contents, Yet, the treaty rule cannot exclude a rule of customary law:

---

24 Vaughan Lowe, "Regulation or Expropriation?" *Current Legal Problems* 55 (2002): 447, 451, 458.

25 Catherine Titi, *Right to Regulate in International Investment Law* (Nomos, 2014), p. 33; Yulia Levashova, *The Right of States to Regulate in International Investment Law: The Search for Balance Between Public Interest and Fair and Equitable Treatment*, (Kluwer Law International, 2019), pp. 26–35.

26 *Gabíkovo-Nagymaros Project (Hungary v Slovakia)*, Judgment, [1997] ICJ Reports 7 (25 September 1997), para. 140; *Questions of Interpretation and Application of the 1971 Montreal Convention arising from the Aerial Incident at Lockerbie (Libyan Arab Jamahiriya v United States of America)*, Judgment, [1998] ICJ Reports 115 (27 February 1998), para. 42.

27 *Jurisdiction of the Courts of Danzig (Pecuniary Claims of Danzig Railway Officials who have Passed into the Polish Service against the Polish Railways Administration)*, Advisory Opinion, PCIJ Series B No. 15 (3 March 1928), 17.

28 *La Grand (Germany v United States of America)*, Judgment, [2001] ICJ Rep. 466 (27 June 2001), 483, 487–88; *United States Diplomatic and Consular Staff in Tehran (United States of America v Iran)*, Judgment, [1980] ICJ Reports 3 (24 May 1980), para. 86.

> It will therefore be clear that customary international law continues to exist and to apply, separately from international treaty law, even where the two categories of law have an identical content.[29]

Additionally, the Court further observed that the incorporation of a customary rule into a treaty does not make the customary rule redundant:

> even if the customary norm and the treaty norm were to have exactly the same content, this would not be a reason for the Court to hold that the incorporation of the customary norm into treaty-law must deprive the customary norm of its applicability as distinct from that of the treaty norm".[30]

These observations are particularly important since the ICJ was interpreting the right of self-defense in Article 51 of the UN Charter and did not see such a multilateral treaty as important as the UN Charter does not replace or supersede the contents of the right of self-defense in customary international law. Rules originating in different sources of international law, such as treaties and customs, are to be interpreted in a compatible manner whereby one assists in the interpretation of another.[31]

In light of above, it would not be correct to suggest that regulatory freedom will be excluded completely once a State enters into an IIA. Unfortunately, few tribunals have taken this position.[32] Also, the tribunals that reject regulatory freedom have not discussed or considered the position of regulatory freedom as a rule of customary international law and its interaction with treaty norms. *Saluka v Czech Republic* clarified the situation greatly. Even where a treaty

29 *Military and Paramilitary Activities in and against Nicaragua (Nicaragua v United States of America)*, Merits, [1986] ICJ Reports 14 (27 June 1986), paras. 177, 179.

30 *Military and Paramilitary Activities in and against Nicaragua (Nicaragua v United States of America)*, Merits, [1986] ICJ Reports 14 (27 June 1986), para. 177.

31 Hugh Thirlway, *The Sources of International Law* (Oxford: Oxford University Press, 2014), 139.

32 *National Grid P.L.C. v. Argentina Republic*, UNCITRAL, Award (3 November 2008), para. 96; *Occidental Petroleum Corporation and Occidental Exploration and Production Company v. Republic of Ecuador*, ICSID Case No. ARB/06/11, Award (5 October 2012), paras. 529–30; *Daimler Financial Services AG v. Argentine Republic*, ICSID Case No. ARB/05/1, Award (22 August 2012), para. 100; *RREEF Infrastructure (G.P.) Limited and RREEF Pan-European Infrastructure Two Lux S.à r.l. v. Kingdom of Spain*, ICSID Case No. ARB/13/30, Decision on Responsibility and on the Principles of Quantum (30 November 2018), paras. 242–3; *Renée Rose Levy de Levi v. Republic of Peru*, ICSID Case No. ARB/10/17, Award (26 February 2014), para. 161.

provision is broadly drafted and does not contain any exception for exercise of regulatory power, yet "the customary international law notion that a deprivation can be justified if it results from the exercise of regulatory actions aimed at the maintenance of public order."[33] The tribunal in *Saluka v Czech Republic* set out the legal principle in the following words:

> It is now established in international law that States are not liable to pay compensation to a foreign investor when, in the normal exercise of their regulatory powers, they adopt in a non-discriminatory manner *bona fide* regulations that are aimed at the general welfare.[34]

This certainly does not mean that the regulatory freedom is absolute.[35]

The possibility of one norm excluding another arises only if they are incompatible that is in a position of conflict. There are detailed principles on how a treaty and customary norm would operate and is a a part of conlict of norms. This is a addressed in the following section.

3 Conflict of Norms

Exclusion of a customary international law rule by a treaty rule is possible if there is a conflict between the two. A conflict exists where compliance with one rule results into violation of another.[36] There must be "direct incompatibility", meaning that a party "cannot simultaneously comply with its obligations."[37] For a situation of conflict to arise, the two rules must cover the same subject matter, have identical contents and one rule exhaustively covers the area without leaving any scope of operation for another rule.[38] Since the exclusion of operation of a rule, particularly a customary international law rule that has

33 *Saluka Investments BV v. The Czech Republic*, Partial Award, PCA Case No. 2001-04, para. 254.

34 *Saluka Investments BV v. The Czech Republic*, Partial Award, PCA Case No. 2001-04, para. 255.

35 *Saluka Investments BV v. The Czech Republic*, Partial Award, PCA Case No. 2001-04, para. 258.

36 Hans Kelsen, *General Theory of Norms*, Michael Hartney trans., (Oxford: Clarendon Press, 1991), 123.

37 Wilferd Jenks, "Conflict of Law Making Treaties," *British Yearbook of International Law* 30 (1953): 401, 425–426.

38 Joost Pauwelyn, *Conflict of Norms in Public International Law: How WTO Law Relates to Other Rules of International Law* (Cambridge: Cambridge University Press, 2003), 164–165.

its own normative value and implicit State consent its exclusion is a serious matter. The presence of a conflict and consequential exclusion of a rule is not to be readily inferred. The notion of conflict itself is to be narrowly interpreted to avoid confrontation between the two rules and to allow them to operate simultaneously.[39] Each of the rules would be interpreted narrowly to ensure that enough space is left for the other rule to operate.[40] Such an approach is particularly important since in certain situations a rule of customary international law may operate as an exception to the treaty rule.[41] If the two rules have exactly the same content yet they can operate alongside each other, they must be given effect. The ICJ explained this point in the *Military and Paramilitary Activities* case in the following words:

> On a number of points, the areas governed by the two sources of law do not exactly overlap, and the substantive rules in which they are framed are not identical in content. But in addition, even if a treaty norm and a customary norm relevant to the present dispute were to have exactly the same content, this would not be a reason for the Court to take the view that the operation of the treaty process must necessarily deprive the customary norm of its separate applicability.[42]

Investment tribunals have applied customary law rules and treaty rules alongside even if they cover the same subject matter. The contents of necessity in customary international law have been applied alongside the treaty rule specifying necessity as a defence from responsibility for breach of an IIA.[43] The

39 *Military and Paramilitary Activities in and against Nicaragua* (*Nicaragua v United States of America*), [1986] ICJ Reports 14 (27 June 1986), para. 178; International Law Commission, Fragmentation of International Law: Difficulties Arising from the Diversification and Expansion of International Law, Report of the Study Group of the International Law Commission, A/CN.4/L.702, Geneva, 1 May–9 June and 3 July–11 August 2006, Part C.

40 Gerald Fitzmaurice, "The Law and Procedure of the International Court of Justice 1951–5: Treaty Interpretation and Other Treaty Points," *British Yearbook of International Law* 33 (1957): 237.

41 *Case Concerning the Difference Between New Zealand and France Concerning the Interpretation or Application of Two Agreements, Concluded on 9 July 1986 Between the Two States and Which Related to the Problem Arising From the Rainbow Warrior Affair* (*New Zealand v France*), Award, Vol. XX RIAA 215 (30 April 1990), paras. 72, 73, 75.

42 *Military and Paramilitary Activities in and against Nicaragua* (*Nicaragua v United States of America*), [1986] ICJ Reports 14 (27 June 1986), para. 175.

43 *CMS Gas Transmission Co. v Argentina*, ICSID Case No. ARB/01/8, Decision on Annulment (25 September 2007), para. 133–134; *Sempra Energy International v The Argentine Republic, Award*, ICSID Case No. ARB/02/16, (28 September 2007), paras 375–378.

exclusion of regulatory freedom as a customary international law rule due to the presence of treatment standards in a treaty would arise only where the treaty clearly excludes or limits the operation of customary international law.

There are additional principles on conflict of norms that would be pertinent to determine whether regulatory freedom is excluded entirely due to treatment standards in IIA. The possibility of exclusion of a customary international law rule by a treaty rule may arise where the treaty rule is *lex specialis* in relation to the customary international law rule.[44] The *lex specialis derogat generali* or simply the *lex specialis* rule is based on the idea that the special rule will supersede the general rule.[45] The *lex specialis* rule does not operate at the regime level. It operates in relation to each of the norms individually. If the two norms in question cover the same subject matter then it is to be seen which norm is specific in the given context.[46] Therefore, it is not open to argue that treatment standards are a part of a specialized regime of international investment law and will supersede regulatory freedom. The pertinent question to ask is whether treatment standards are specific as opposed to regulatory freedom. States adopt a wide range of measures. Not all of them fall within the purview of regulatory freedom. For a measure to fall within the purview of regulatory freedom it has to satisfy the requirements of customary international law. Investment treaties do not bar exercise of regulatory freedom or exercise of all measures. Losses arising out of legitimate regulatory exercise are not treated to constitute violation of treatment standards.[47] Investment treaties are silent on the issue of regulatory freedom. The only place where the rules regulating regulatory freedom can be found are in customary international law. Therefore, on the issue of laws regulating exercise of regulatory freedom, especially whether a measure falls within regulatory freedom, the appropriate place to look for is customary international law. To that extent, customary

44 *Dispute Concerning Access to Information under Article 9 of the OSPAR Convention (Ireland v United Kingdom of Great Britain and Northern Ireland)*, Award, (2005) 126 ILR 364 (2 July 2003), para. 84; Joost Pauwelyn, *Conflict of Norms in Public International Law: How WTO Law Relates to Other Rules of International Law* (Cambridge: Cambridge University Press, 2003), 271.

45 Michael Akehurst, "The Hierarchy of the Sources of International Law," *British Yearbook of International Law* 47 (1975): 274, 274.

46 *Gabíkovo-Nagymaros Project (Hungary v Slovakia)*, Judgment, [1997] ICJ Reports 7 (25 September 1997),132; Bruno Simma and Dirk Pulkowski, "Of Planets and Universe: Self-contained Regimes in International Law," *European Journal of International Law* 17 (2006): 483, 487–489.

47 International Law Commission, *Draft Articles on State Responsibility with Commentaries Thereto, Adopted by the International Law Commission on First Reading* 1997, A/56/10, art. 5 (referring to the Harvard Draft).

international law rules on regulatory freedom operate as *lex specialis* in relation to the treatment standards. Treatment standards restrict the 'manner' of exercise of sovereign power of a State. The rules on regulatory freedom in customary international law also have the same goal, that is they protect only those measures that fall within a certain 'manner' of function. Therefore, treatment standards and regulatory freedom are complementary rather than competing. A State action is unlawful if it causes injury to an alien "without sufficient justification" and the injury is intended or caused.[48] Measures taken for protecting public order, health, or morality are sufficient justifications.[49]

Where a conflict of norms exists, the norm of primary importance would abrogate another norm to the extent of incompatibility. If there is absolute incompatibility then the other norm is completely derogated but if the incompatibility is partial the rest of the original norm continues to operate.[50] A conflict or displacement is not to be readily inferred. Therefore, if there is divergence amongst two norms, they could be reconciled by adjusting their scope to avoid conflict during interpretation.[51] The presence of treatment standards would not allow States absolute sovereign discretion to act in any manner. Instead the freedom of States would be limited to legitimate regulations undertaken in public interest.

To say that the mere presence of a treaty disallows the use of customary law right of regulatory freedom would amount to presuming the presence of a conflict. But the starting point for dealing with norms originating in two different sources is the presumption of absence of conflict.[52] The goal of investment treaties is to protect foreign investors but at the same time allow States to undertake reasonable measures. A balanced approach that allows for the concurrent application of regulatory freedom and treatment standards was advocated in the following words in *Saluka v Czech Republic*:

---

48 International Law Commission, *Draft Articles on State Responsibility with Commentaries Thereto, Adopted by the International Law Commission on First Reading 1997*, A/56/10, art. 3.1(a) (referring to the Harvard Draft).

49 International Law Commission, *Draft Articles on State Responsibility with Commentaries Thereto, Adopted by the International Law Commission on First Reading 1997*, A/56/10 art. 4.2 (referring to the Harvard Draft).

50 Hans Kelsen, *General Theory of Norms*, Michael Hartney trans., (Oxford: Clarendon Press, 1991), 111–112.

51 International Law Commission, Report of the Study Group of the International Law Commission, Fragmentation of International Law: Difficulties Arising From the Diversification and Expansion of International Law, A/CN.4/L.682 (2006), para. 43.

52 Hersh Lauterpact, ed., *Oppenheim's International Law*, 7th ed., vol. 1 (1948), 858–859; Wilferd Jenks, "Conflict of Law Making Treaties," *British Yearbook of International Law* 30 (1953): 401,428.

> This is a more subtle and balanced statement of the Treaty's aims than is sometimes appreciated. The protection of foreign investments is not the sole aim of the Treaty, but rather a necessary element alongside the overall aim of encouraging foreign investment and extending and intensifying the parties' economic relations. That in turn calls for a balanced approach to the interpretation of the Treaty's substantive provisions for the protection of investments, since an interpretation which exaggerates the protection to be accorded to foreign investments may serve to dissuade host States from admitting foreign investments and so undermine the overall aim of extending and intensifying the parties' mutual economic relations[53]

As noted in the paragraph quoted above, regulatory freedom is not entirely excluded, rather it continues to operate alongside treatment standards. The approach of international courts and tribunals also supports this position. Of particular importance are decisions of international courts and tribunals on the relationship between a norm in a treaty and customary international law, generally under international law and specifically on the question of regulatory freedom. The following section turns to that discussion.

4 Jurisprudence of International Courts and Tribunals

International courts and tribunals have reconciled regulatory freedom with treaty obligations and found that if the elements of regulatory freedom as contained in customary international law are satisfied they would not constitute breach of a treaty. Even where the treaty covers the same area as customary international law, regulatory freedom continues to operate. These decisions are pertinent for investment arbitration because they have extensively explored the relationship between a treaty and customary international law obligation. They have been consistent, indicating *jurisprudence constant*. Moreover, as elaborated investment tribunals and international investment law does not or cannot exist in seclusion from general international law.

In the *North Atlantic Coast Fisheries* case, the issue was whether Great Britain had retained regulatory freedom over fishing after granting exclusive and perpetual fishing rights to the United States under the treaty of 1818. The

53 *Saluka Investments BV v. The Czech Republic*, PCA Case No. 2001-04, Partial Award (17 March 2006), para.300.

tribunal found that regulatory freedom was not extinguished by the treaty. The treaty required that regulatory freedom is to be exercised reasonably.[54] There is no need to expressly mention regulatory freedom in a treaty to preserve it. It is always present and its exclusion cannot be presumed.[55] Summarizing the position, the tribunal held that:

> In any event, Great Britain, as the local sovereign, has the duty of preserving and protecting the fisheries. In so far as it is necessary for that purpose, Great Britain is not only entitled, but obliged, to provide for the protection and preservation of the fisheries; always remembering that the exercise of this right of legislation is limited by the obligation to execute the Treaty in good faith.[56]

Most importantly, the US argued that it was not possible to draw a precise 'line' between regulatory freedom and treaty obligations.[57] The tribunal in *Saluka v Czech Republic* expressed a similar concern, despite acknowledging the presence of regulatory freedom in the following words:

> international law has yet to identify in a comprehensive and definitive fashion precisely what regulations are considered "permissible" and "commonly accepted" as falling within the police or regulatory power of States and, thus, non-compensable. In other words, it has yet to draw a bright and easily distinguishable line between non-compensable regulations on the one hand and, on the other, measures that have the effect of depriving foreign investors of their investment and are thus unlawful and compensable in international law.[58]

This view is echoed by other tribunals and scholars, and they have argued that since it is not possible to draw a diving line between regulatory freedom and

---

54 *The North Atlantic Coast Fisheries case* (*Great Britain v United States of America*), Award, (1961) 11 RIAA 167 (7 September 1910), 181–185.

55 *The North Atlantic Coast Fisheries case* (*Great Britain v United States of America*), Award, (1961) 11 RIAA 167 (7 September 1910), 186.

56 *The North Atlantic Coast Fisheries case* (*Great Britain v United States of America*), Award, (1961) 11 RIAA 167 (7 September 1910), 187.

57 *The North Atlantic Coast Fisheries case* (*Great Britain v United States of America*), Award, (1961) 11 RIAA 167 (7 September 1910), 188.

58 *Saluka Investments B.V. v. The Czech Republic*, UNCITRAL, Partial Award, 17 March 2006, para. 263.

breaches of the treaty the matter is entirely within the discretion of the tribunal and decision will have to be made on a case-by-case basis.[59]

The US argument in the *North Atlantic Coast Fisheries* case was rejected by the arbitral tribunal. The tribunal held that the so-called difficulty in drawing a 'line' is irrelevant because regulatory freedom and treaty obligations operate in two distinct spheres. Regulatory freedom is restrained to the extent that the regulations are made in good faith (*bona fide*).[60] The scope of operation and regulatory freedom is different from treaty obligations because once a measure satisfies the requirements under customary international law to become a regulatory measure by their very nature those measures do not breach treatment standards. In his comments on this case McNair summed up the effects of a treaty on regulatory freedom in the following words:

> the right of a State to regulate the enjoyment by another State of rights derived from a treaty or from customary international law must be exercised reasonably and in good faith and not in such a way as to destroy the effective enjoyment of those rights.[61]

Thus, it is possible to distinguish between the two and the division is clear.

It is not that the presence of a treaty is inconsequential. The effect of the presence of the treaty is that regulatory freedom is to be exercised reasonably and in good faith.

The ICJ had the opportunity to comment on the relationship between regulatory freedom and treaty obligations in the *Navigation Rights* case. The issue before the Court was whether in light of a treaty obligation, Nicaragua retained and if it did then to what extent the right to regulate navigation over the San Juan river, after having transferred the right of navigation in favour of Costa Rica

59 *Generation Ukraine Incorporation v Ukraine*, ICSID Case No. ARB/00/9, Award (16 September 2003), para 20.29; Jan Paulsson and Zachary Douglas, "Indirect Expropriation in Investment Treaty Arbitration" in *Arbitrating Foreign Investment Disputes: Procedural and Substantive Legal Aspects*, ed. Norbert Horn and Stephan Kroll (The Hague: Kluwer Law International, 2004), p. 146; Jan Paulsson, "Indirect Expropriation: Is the Right to Regulate at Risk?" Paper presented on 12 December 2005 in Paris at a symposium on 'Making the Most of International Investment Agreements' organized by ICSID, OECD and UNCTAD, pp. 1–2 (available at http://www.oecd.org/investment/internationalinvestmentagreements/36055332.pdf; accessed 18 June 2024); see generally L Yves Fortier and Stephen L Drymer, "Indirect Expropriation in the Law of International Investment: I Know It When I See It, or *Caveat Investor*" *ICSID Review-FILJ* 19 (2004): 29.

60 *The North Atlantic Coast Fisheries case* (*Great Britain v United States of America*), Award, (1961) XI RIAA 167 (7 September 1910), 188–189.

61 Arnold McNair, *The Law of Treaties* (2nd ed; Oxford: Clarendon Press, 1961), p. 764.

under the treaty of 1958. The rights granted to Costa Rica by Nicaragua under the treaty were general and open-ended. They covered navigational rights for commercial purposes: "libre navegación ... con objetos de comercio".[62] These rights allowed Costa Rica to exercise regulatory freedom on matters of navigation and commerce over the San Juan river.[63] Nicaragua argued that despite the treaty where the right to regulate navigation and commerce were transferred to Costa Rica, it retained extensive rights to regulate operations on the San Juan river. Initially the parties disagreed about the existence of regulatory freedom in light of the treaty but as the matter proceeded to the merits stage, the parties agreed that the right to regulate was present and the dispute was limited to the scope of that right. The Court noted the agreement of the parties in the following words:

> It states that the regulations must be lawful, public, reasonable, non-arbitrary and non-discriminatory, and adopted to fulfill a legitimate public purpose. Nicaragua accepts Costa Rica's statement of principle.[64]

The Court noted that the provisions of a treaty limiting sovereignty is not to be restrictively interpreted but at the same time it is not to be interpreted liberally in favour of the party claiming rights under the treaty. According to the Court and most importantly, "limitations of the sovereignty of a State over its territory are not to be presumed."[65] The act of entering into a treaty precludes the argument of absolute discretion of a State to take measures it likes. A treaty 'tempers' those rights but does not dislodge them entirely: According to the Court

> the power to regulate ... is not unlimited, being tempered by the rights and obligations of the Parties.[66]

62 *Dispute regarding Navigational and Related Rights* (*Costa Rica v. Nicaragua*), Judgment, (2009) ICJ Reports 213 (13 July 2009), para. 19.

63 *Dispute regarding Navigational and Related Rights* (*Costa Rica v. Nicaragua*), Judgment, (2009) ICJ Reports 213 (13 July 2009), para. 32.

64 *Dispute regarding Navigational and Related Rights* (*Costa Rica v. Nicaragua*), Judgment, (2009) ICJ Reports 213 (13 July 2009), para. 86.

65 *Dispute regarding Navigational and Related Rights* (*Costa Rica v. Nicaragua*), Judgment, (2009) ICJ Reports 213 (13 July 2009), para. 48.

66 *Dispute regarding Navigational and Related Rights* (*Costa Rica v. Nicaragua*), Judgment, (2009) ICJ Reports 213 (13 July 2009), para. 87.

The Court identified the following elements of regulatory freedom: "a legitimate purpose"; "must not be discriminatory", "it must not be unreasonable, which means that its negative impact on the exercise of the right in question must not be manifestly excessive when measured against the protection afforded to the purpose invoked."[67]

Furthermore, the Court observed that the obligations under a treaty cannot be fixed in time and regulatory freedom has to be interpreted in an evolutionary manner.[68] In the words of the Court:

> The Court considers that, over the course of the century and a half since the 1858 Treaty was concluded, the interests which are to be protected through regulation in public interest may well have changed in ways that could never have been anticipated by the Parties at the time: protecting the environment is a notable example. ... Nicaragua, in adopting certain measure which have been challenged, in the Court's opinion, is pursuing the legitimate purpose of protecting the environment.[69]

The need to take into account changes in various fields of international law, particularly environmental law while interpreting a treaty were also emphasized by the Court in the *Gabčíkovo-Nagymaros Project* case.[70] There is no reason why the principles on the relationship between regulatory freedom and treaty obligations as developed in the jurisprudence of international courts and tribunals shall not be applied to the relationship between regulatory freedom and treatment standards in IIAs.

If a measure satisfies the requirements of regulatory freedom under customary international law, it operates without overlapping or infringing the treaty obligation of treatment standards. Neither do the treatment standards in IIAs expressly exclude regulatory freedom not they operate in a manner that regulatory freedom would be excluded by implication. Regulatory freedom and treatment standards govern two distinct areas.

67 *Dispute regarding Navigational and Related Rights* (*Costa Rica v. Nicaragua*), Judgment, (2009) ICJ Reports 213 (13 July 2009), para. 87.

68 *Dispute regarding Navigational and Related Rights* (*Costa Rica v. Nicaragua*), Judgment, (2009) ICJ Reports 213 (13 July 2009), para. 89.

69 *Dispute regarding Navigational and Related Rights* (*Costa Rica v. Nicaragua*), Judgment, (2009) ICJ Reports 213 (13 July 2009), para. 89.

70 *Gabíkovo-Nagymaros Project* (*Hungary v Slovakia*), Judgment, [1997] ICJ Rep. 7 (25 September 1997), para. 140. Followed in *The Indus Waters Kishenganga Arbitration* (*Pakistan v. India*), Permanent Court of Arbitration, Final Award, (20 December 2013), para 85.

The framework of the discussion until now is applied to assess the relationship between regulatory freedom and specific treatment standards in the following chapters. The following chapters take a closer look at the interaction of regulatory freedom with some prominent treatment standards and seeks if regulatory freedom is compatible with those treatment standards in light of the interpretations provided by investment tribunals. Also, whether and to what extent those treatment standards limit regulatory freedom.

CHAPTER 4

Regulatory Freedom and Expropriation

This chapter focuses on the relationship between regulatory freedom and expropriation, particularly the operation of indirect expropriation which has created difficulties in delineating whether a measure can be treated as regulatory freedom or indirect expropriation.

Expropriation is one of the oldest treatment standards for the protection of foreign investment. It existed in the Friendship Commerce and Navigation (FCN) treaties and is present in almost all IIAs.[1] The FCN treaties only contained 'direct' expropriation. However, the scope of expropriation provisions in IIAs is broader than direct expropriation. It includes other types of expropriation particularly indirect expropriation. The Canada-EU Free Trade Agreement (CETA) provide a relatively recent example of a standard expropriation clause:

> A Party shall not nationalise or expropriate a covered investment either directly, or indirectly through measures having an effect equivalent to nationalisation or expropriation ('expropriation')[2]

The interpretation of an expropriation clause, especially the scope and mutual effect of various types of expropriations covered in the expropriation clause will affect the scope of regulatory freedom. If the expropriation clause and the various types of expropriation covered by that clause are interpreted broadly, the scope of regulatory freedom will be reduced. And, the vice-versa will also be true. It is therefore necessary firstly to investigate the types of expropriations covered under the expropriation clause and their scope.

Direct expropriation, referred to as 'expropriation' or 'nationalization' is the situation where the State takes the property or directs the property to be transferred to another beneficiary. There is a direct transfer of property and is best captured in the word 'taking'. Expropriation or taking may be a part of

---

1 Campbell McLachlan, Laurence Shore & Matthew Weiniger, *International Investment Arbitration: Substantive Principles* (Oxford: Oxford University Press, 2007), 266–267; Kenneth Vandevelde, *Bilateral Investment Treaties: History, Policy and Interpretation* (New York: Oxford University Press, 2010), 282.

2 EU-Canada Comprehensive Economic and Trade Agreement (CETA) (2016), art. 8.12(1); Energy Charter Treaty, 2080 UNTS 95 (17 December 1994), art. 13(1).

 | DOI:10.1163/9789004759831_005

the broader government policy or involves specific instances of taking of property. Normally, the term expropriation is broad and it includes all instances of transfer of property, whereas nationalization is specific and covers situations of transfer of assets to the government as a part of a programme to take over assets in a given sector or in a given situation.[3] Thus a nationalisation is expropriation but every expropriation may not constitute nationalisation. Instances of direct taking are rare, if not absent and the State is responsible to compensate as per the conditions contained in the IIA. A State cannot rely on regulatory freedom and cannot escape from the responsibility for payment of compensation for the losses caused to the foreign investor because the State promises to compensate if it takes actions whereby the States takes the property.

In the case of indirect expropriation – also known as *de facto* expropriation – the investor may continue to remain in control of the investment, but the investment may have become valueless or reductant due to the measures of a host State.[4] In *Techmed v Mexico*, the tribunal explained indirect expropriation in the following words:

> Although formally an expropriation means a forcible taking by the Government of tangible or intangible property owned by private persons by means of administrative or legislative action to that effect, the term also covers a number of situations defined as de facto expropriation, where such actions or laws transfer the assets to third parties different from the expropriating State or where such laws or actions deprive persons of their ownership over such assets without allocating such assets to third parties.[5]

3 B A Wortley, *Expropriation in International Law* (Cambridge: Cambridge University Press, 1959), p. 36; Konstantin Katzarov, *The Theory of Nationalisation* (The Hague: Martinus Nijhoff, 1964), pp. 1–2, 141–2; Gillian White, *Nationalization of Foreign Property* (London: Stevens & Sons Limited, 1961), p. 43; Aniruddha Rajput, *Regulatory Freedom and Indirect Expropriation in Investment Arbitration* (Kluwer International, 2018), pp. 21–3.

4 August Reinisch, 'Expropriation' in *The Oxford Handbook of International Investment Law*, ed. Peter Muchlinski, Frederico Ortino and Christoph Schreuer (Oxford: Oxford University Press, 2008), pp. 421–3 (footnotes excluded); Christoph Schreuer, "The Concept of Expropriation under the ECT and other Investment Protection Treaties" in *Investment Arbitration and the Energy Charter Treaty*, ed. Clarisse Ribeiro (Juris Publishing, 2006), pp. 126–33.

5 *Medioambientales Techmed S.A. v The United Mexican States*, Award, ICSID Case No. ARB (AF)/00/2 (29 May 2003), para 113 (foot note omitted).

CETA defines indirect expropriation as "measures having an effect equivalent to nationalisation or expropriation ('expropriation')". Other IIAs include similar formulations: 'equivalent to expropriation',[6] 'tantamount to expropriation'[7] or 'effect equivalent to expropriation'.[8]

Another factual description of certain measures, although not expressly mentioned in IIAs, but very much included within the umbrella of indirect expropriation is 'creeping expropriation'. The tribunal in *Generation Ukraine v Ukraine* defined creeping expropriation in the following words:

> Creeping expropriation is a form of indirect expropriation with a distinctive temporal quality in the sense that it encapsulates the situation whereby a series of acts attributable to the State over a period of time culminate in the expropriatory taking of such property.[9]

6 Mexico-UK BIT (signed 12 May 2006, entered into force 25 July 2007) Art. 7; Canada-Slovakia (signed 20 July 2010, entered into force 14 March 2012) Art. VI.1; Netherlands-Oman BIT (signed 17 January 2009) Art. 4; Japan-Cambodia BIT (signed 14 June 2007, entered into force 31 July 2008) Art. 12(1); US-Uruguay BIT (signed 4 November 2005, entered into force 31 October 2006) Art. 6; Russia-Egypt BIT (signed 23 September 1997) Art. VI.]

7 Egypt-Germany BIT (signed 16 June 2005, entered into force 22 November 2009) Art. 4; Japan-Lao People's Democratic Republic BIT (signed 16 January 2008, entered into force 3 August 2008) Art. 12; Egypt-Japan BIT (signed 28 January 1977, entered into force 14 January 1978) Art. 5; Japan-Vietnam BIT (signed 14 November 2003, entered into force 19 December 2004) Art. 9; Japan Turkey BIT (signed 12 February 1992, entered into force 12 March 1993) Art. 5(2); Japan-Egypt BIT (signed 28 January 1977, entered into force 14 January 1978) Art. 5(2); US-Congo BIT (signed 12 February 1990, entered into force 13 August 1994) Art. III; US-Honduras BIT (signed 1 July 1995, entered into force 11 July 2001) Art. III; US-Turkey BIT (signed 3 December 1985, entered into force 18 May 1990) Art. III.

8 UK-Sierra Leone BIT (signed 13 January 2000, entered into force 20 November 2001) Art. 5. These provisions expressly incorporate neutralization requirement, which is implicit in the second category; Energy Charter Treaty (signed 17 December 1994, entered into force 30 September 1999) Art. 13(1); Agreement for the Promotion and Reciprocal Protection of Investments (Canada-Ecuador) (signed on 29 April 1996, entered into force 6 June 1997) Art. VIII. 1; Agreement for the Promotion and Protection of Investments (Argentina-United Kingdom) (11 December 1990) Art. 5(1); Mexico-UK BIT, 2006 (signed on 12 May 2006, entered into force 25 July 2007) Art. 7; Canada-Slovakia BIT (signed on 20 July 2010, entered into force 14 March 2012) Art. VI.1; Burundi-Netherlands BIT (signed on 24 May 2007) 'effect equivalent to expropriation'.

9 *Generation Ukraine, Inc. v Ukraine, Award,* ICSID Case No. ARB/00/9 (16 September 2003), para. 20.22; M. Sornarajah, *The International Law on Foreign Investment* (3rd ed., Cambridge: Cambridge University Press, 2010), p. 369; August Reinisch, "Expropriation" in *The Oxford Handbook of International Investment Law*, ed. Peter Muchlinski, Frederico Ortino and Christoph Schreuer (Oxford: Oxford University Press, 2008), pp. 426–7 (footnotes excluded).

It has been suggested in scholarship that the objective of various categories of expropriation and especially creeping expropriation[10] is to expand the scope of expropriation clauses to include all losses suffered by the investor due to measure of the government – irrespective of the nature of those measures.[11] Most investment tribunals have rejected such arguments. They have held that the presence of indirect expropriation is a reason to expand the meaning of expropriation.[12] Likewise, creeping expropriation does not allow expansion of the interpretation of the expropriation provisions in IIAs.[13] There are some rare exceptions of tribunals where the expansive effect has be proposed. In *Metalclad v Mexico* the tribunal was one such. It supported the view that the scope of the expropriation clause was widened due to the presence of other types of expropriation.[14] This interpretation was criticized by the Supreme Court of British Columbia when the award was challenged (although the finding was not set aside due to the limits on review jurisdiction).[15] The tribunal in *Waste Management v Mexico* was circumspect. It supported the expansive approach only due to the context rather than the text of the treaty it was interpreting. The tribunal was careful to clarify that this interpretation would not

10 W. Michael Reisman & Robert D. Sloane, "Indirect Expropriation and Its Valuation in the BIT Generation," *British Yearbook of International Law* 74 (2003): 115, 128.

11 Rudolf Dolzer & Margarete Stevens, *Bilateral Investment Treaties* (Hague: Martinus Nijhoff Publishers, 1995), 102; Jeswald W Salacuse, *The Law of Investment Treaties* (New York: Oxford University Press, 2010), p. 293–294.

12 *Telenor Mobile Communications S.A. v The Republic of Hungary*, Award, ICSID Case No. ARB/04/15 (13 September 2006), para. 63; *Pope & Talbot Inc. v The Government of Canada*, Interim Award, UNCITRAL (26 June 2000), paras 83–84, 92; *S.D. Myers, Inc. v Government of Canada*, Partial Award (13 November 2000), para. 286; *Técnicas Medioambientales Tecmed, S.A. v. The United Mexican States*, ICSID Case No. ARB (AF)/00/2, para. 114.

13 *S.D. Myers, Inc. v Government of Canada*, Partial Award (13 November 2000), para. 286.

14 *Metalclad Corporation v. The United Mexican States*, Case No. ARB(AF)/97/1, Award (30 August 2000), paras. 102–103.

15 *The United Mexican States v Metaclad Corporation*, Reasons for the Judgment of the Honourable Mr Justice Tysoe, The Supreme Court of British Columbia, (2001) BCSC 664, para. 99. According to Tyose J: 'The Tribunal gave an extremely broad definition of expropriation for the purposes of Article 1110. In addition to the more conventional notion of expropriation involving a taking of property, the Tribunal held that expropriation under the NAFTA includes covert or incidental interference with the use of property which has the effect of depriving the owner, in whole or in significant part, of the use or reasonably-to-be-expected economic benefit of property. This definition is sufficiently broad to include a legitimate rezoning of property by a municipality or other zoning authority. However, the definition of expropriation is a question of law with which this Court is not entitled to interfere under the International CAA.'

extent to other treaties.[16] It is noteworthy that the tribunal clarified that the expansion of the scope of expropriation clauses due to the presence of different types of expropriation does not cover regulatory freedom, which States continue to enjoy without attracting responsibility for breach of the expropriation standard.[17]

In *Marvin Feldman v Mexico* it was clarified that the categories of indirect expropriation are "functionally equivalent" rather than distinct categories.[18] The reference to 'functionally equivalent' indicates that the nature of all the different types of expropriation has to be that of an expropriatory measure. The expropriation standard in IIAs cannot be widened due to the presence of different types of expropriatory measures to cover, and consequentially hold States responsible for regulatory measures. States have also issued clarifications stating that the different categories of expropriation do not create a higher standard.[19]

A convincing interpretation, emerging from the text of the IIAs is that the effect of the measure has to be the same that would be caused by expropriation or nationalization. All types of losses caused due to the measure of a State are not intended to be included in expropriation provisions. The expropriation clauses make it clear that indirect expropriation is a "measures having an effect equivalent to nationalisation or expropriation". The focus of the different categories of expropriation is on the 'effect'. They do not refer to general effects or all effects of measures. They focus only on effects that would have the same effect of expropriation or nationalization, hence the reference to the terms 'equivalent to' or 'tantamount to' expropriation. This interpretation is reaffirmed, in IIAs such as CETA and ECT, with a reference to 'expropriation' in the bracket. Therefore, it is necessary to look at the nature of the measure to decide if the effect caused is due to a measure that is expropriatory in nature

16 *Waste Management Inc. v United Mexican States*, Award, ICSID Case No. ARB(AF)/00/3 (30 April 2004), paras 143–145.

17 *Waste Management Inc. v United Mexican States*, Award, ICSID Case No. ARB(AF)/00/3 (30 April 2004), para. 155.

18 *Marvin Roy Feldman Karpa v. United Mexican States*, ICSID Case No. ARB(AF)/99/1 (16 December 2002), para. 100; *Petrobart Limited v The Kyrgyz Republic*, Arbitration Institute of the Stockholm Chamber of Commerce Case No. 126/2003, Award (29 March 2005), p. 77.

19 Treaty Concerning the Encouragement and Reciprocal Protection of Investment (Bolivia-United States) (signed 17 April 1988, entered into force 6 June 2001) Art. III.1; Treaty Concerning the Encouragement and Reciprocal Protection of Investment (United States-Jordan) (signed 2 July 1997, entered into force 13 June 2003) Art. XII; Campbell McLachlan, Laurence Shore & Matthew Weiniger, *International Investment Arbitration: Substantive Principles* (Oxford: Oxford University Press, 2007), 276–280.

or is regulatory. Several treaties belonging to later generation make the distinction between an expropriatory and regulatory measure and clarify that the categories of expropriation are limited to expropriatory measures.[20] In order to understand how to distinguish between a measure that constitutes expropriation and others that do not, it is necessary to understand the conceptual difference between a regulatory measure and an expropriatory measure. To a large extent, this distinction is foundational and provides the conceptual framework to distinguish the two. The following section turns to the distinction between the regulatory and expropriatory measure.

1 Regulatory Measure Versus Expropriatory Measure

The major challenge faced by investment tribunals is to distinguish between a regulatory measure and an expropriatory measure. Both are ultimately a 'measure' of the State affect the foreign investor, but a State is not responsible to compensate for the former and responsible to compensate in the case of the latter. In the absence of this distinction, States would be responsible to compensate for all losses. Equally, to the contrary, States would not be responsible to compensate for any losses if all measures of the State are treated as regulatory measures. This issue become acute with indirect expropriation since now a days there is no direct taking by States and if the basis to compensate the foreign investor is solely a loss of value of the investment, there is a possibility that every measure that causes loss would be treated as indirect expropriation.

The difference between a regulatory measure and an expropriatory measure is well-established in international law as well as municipal law. Like in international law, regulatory freedom is referred to as 'police powers' in municipal law and distinguished from an expropriatory measure which is called 'eminent domain' or 'taking'. However, the genesis and contents of regulatory freedom (or police powers) is different in municipal law than in international law. The doctrine of eminent domain arose out of the concept that the ruler is the ultimate owner of all lands with absolute authority. In international law the distinction between the regulatory and expropriatory measures arouse

20 US-Australia FTA (signed 18 May 2004, entered into force 1 January 2005) Art. 11.7; US-Chile FTA (signed 6 June 2003, entered into force 1 January 2004) Annexure 10-A; Letter Annexed to the US-Singapore FTA, signed 6 May 2003, entered into force 1 January 2004; Canada-Peru FTA (signed on 29 May 2008, came into force on 1 August 2009) Annexure 812.1; India-Slovenia BIT (signed 14 June 2011) Protocol; India-Malaysia FTA (signed 18 February 2011) Annex 10; China-India BIT (signed 21 November 2006) Protocol; Canada-Slovakia BIT (signed 20 July 2010) Annex A.

out of the treatment of aliens and the freedom of States to exercise sovereign authority over the aliens when the aliens are within their jurisdiction.[21]

The decisive factor in distinguishing a regulatory measure from an expropriatory measure is the objective behind the measure in question. The aim of an expropriatory measure is to 'take' the property. Taking may take place either directly or indirectly: that is the government may direct that the property is to be transferred to itself or to a third party beneficiary. There is unjust enrichment in favour of the State or the beneficiaries intended by the State at the cost of the private entity.[22] This point was well explained in *Olguin v Paraguay* in the following words:

> For an expropriation to occur, there must be actions that can be considered reasonably appropriate for producing the effect of depriving the affected party of the property it owns, in such a way that whoever performs those actions will acquire, directly or indirectly, control, or at least the fruits of the expropriated property. Expropriation therefore requires teleologically driven action for it to occur; omissions, however egregious they may be, are not sufficient for it to take place.[23]

On the other hand, the aim of a regulatory measure is to achieve a public purpose and not to take or harm private property. The effect, if any, on the property is unintended or collateral. The property is neither taken by the State nor transferred to a third entity thus there is no unjust enrichment.

Even where a State does not acquire property but simply destroys the property that too would fall within the purview of an expropriatory measure. The focus of an expropriatory measure is on the severance of title over the property. Post severance, the property may be taken by the State, transferred to

---

21 Aniruddha Rajput, *Regulatory Freedom and Indirect Expropriation in Investment Arbitration* (Kluwer International, 2018), pp. 10–13, 17–18.

22 *S. D. Myers, Inc. v Government of Canada*, UNCITRAL, Separate Opinion by Dr Bryan Schwartz (on the Partial Award) (12 November 2000), para. 212; Christoph Schreuer, "Unjustified Enrichment in International Law," American Journal of Comparative Law 22 (1974): 281, 283–287; Christina Binder & Christoph Schreuer, "Unjust Enrichment" in *Max Planck Encyclopedia of Public International Law*, ed. Rüdiger Wolfrum (New York: Oxford University Press, 2008), para 13.

23 *Eudoro Armando Olguín v Republic of Paraguay*, Award, ICSID Case No. ARB/98/5 (26 January 2001), para. 84; Brownlie also describes expropriation as a process where, 'deprivation may be followed by transfer to the territorial State or to the third parties, as in systems of land distribution as a means of agrarian reform'. Ian Brownlie, *Principles of Public International Law* (7th ed., Oxford: Oxford University Press, 2008), 532 (footnotes omitted).

third-party or destroyed. The severance of ownership may be achieved through various forms. If it is done by the State directly, it is direct expropriation. If the severance is achieved indirectly, then, it is indirect expropriation.[24] The destruction of property may either be direct or by creating situations that force severance of the relationship with the property.[25] There can be no public interest in simply destroying property of private persons for vindictive or colourable exercise of authority. The destruction of property is also a type of severance of the title over the property.[26]

In the exercise of regulatory freedom, no effort is made to severe the relationship of title over the ownership. As explained by Wortley and other scholars the goal of an expropriatory measure is to cause economic injury but incidental losses do not constitute expropriation since, as it a "a mere incident of lawful exercise of police powers".[27]

Since in the case of an expropriatory measure the intention is to severe the relationship of the owner to the property, the losses are visible and quantifiable, subject to the principles of valuation. But in the case of a regulatory measure the impact is subjective. The principal aim of the measure is not to cause damage to the property hence the losses suffered are indirect and that quantification is a complex process unless a taking. The aspects of partial takin are not entirely helpful in these situations. While exercising regulatory freedom a State is performing its functions as an independent arbiter but through an expropriatory measure it is enriching itself or somebody else.[28] The difference in the process and outcome of a regulatory measure and expropriatory measure was expressed in the separate opinion of one of the arbitrators in *SD Myers v. Canada* in the following words:

24 B.A. Wortley, *Expropriation in International Law* (Cambridge: Cambridge University Press, 1959), p. 1.

25 International Law Commission, International Responsibility, Fourth Report by F.V. García Amador, Special Rapporteur: Responsibility of the State for Injuries Caused in its Territory to the Person or Property of Aliens – Measures Affecting Acquired Rights Document (26 February 1959) UN Doc A/CN.4/119, (1959) II Yearbook of the International Law Commission 1, para. 46.

26 *Antoine Biloune, Marine Drive Complex Ltd. v Ghana Investments Centre, the Government of Ghana*, Awards (27 October 1989), (1994) XIX Yearbook Commercial Arbitration 11, 12–3.

27 B.A. Wortley, *Expropriation in International Law* (Cambridge: Cambridge University Press, 1959), p. 50–53; Joseph Sax, "Takings and the Police Power" (1964) *Yale Law Journal* 36, 36; Ian Brownlie, *Principles of Public International Law* (7th ed., Oxford: Oxford University Press, 2008), p. 532.

28 Frank Michelman, "Property, Utility, and Fairness: Comments on the Ethical Foundations of the "Just Compensation" Law" *Harvard Law Review* 80 (1967): 1165, 1200–1201; Joseph Sax, "Takings and the Police Power" (1964) *Yale Law Journal* 36, 60.

> Expropriations tend to deprive the owner and to enrich – by a corresponding amount – the public authority that the property, or the third party to whom the property is given. There is both unfair deprivation and unjust enrichment when an expropriation is carried out with compensation. By contrast, regulatory action tends to prevent an owner from using property in a way that unjustly enriches the owner. For example, an unregulated manufacturing operation might make more money by not bothering to reduce the amount of pollution it sends into the wider community. The government that imposes the regulation does not necessarily profit from its intervention; indeed, it may be expensive to both enact and administer regulations.[29]

Since 'deprivation' is the common element in an expropriatory as well as a regulatory measure, the notion of 'deprivation' , as noted by the tribunal in *Saluka v Czech Republic*,has to be "understood in the meaning it has acquired in customary international law."[30] As per customary international law "a State does not commit an expropriation and is thus not liable to pay compensation to a dispossessed alien investor when it adopts general regulations that are "commonly accepted as within the police power of States" forms part of customary international law today."[31] The tribunal in *El Paso v Argentina* acknowledged that there is a clear distinction between "deprivation amounting to expropriation and interference with property by regulations not amounting to expropriation".[32]

The difference between an expropriatory and a regulatory measure can be best explained with an example. Let us say, to achieve net carbon zero emission a State introduces obligatory technology standards for car manufacturers. As a result, all manufacturers would suffer economic injury due to the costs involved in moving to higher technology standards and the losses they suffer would be to a different degree based on the level of technology that they

29 *S.D. Myers, Inc. v Government of Canada*, UNCITRAL, Separate Opinion by Dr Bryan Schwartz (on the Partial Award) (12 November 2000), para. 212; for similar reasoning see *Petrobart Limited v. The Kyrgyz Republic*, Arbitral Award, CC Case No. 126/2003 (29 March 2005), p. 77.

30 *Saluka Investments BV v. The Czech Republic*, PCA Case No. 2001-04 (17 March 2006), para. 261.

31 *Saluka Investments BV v. The Czech Republic*, PCA Case No. 2001-04 (17 March 2006), para. 262.

32 *El Paso Energy International Company v. The Argentine Republic*, ICSID Case No. ARB/03/15, Award (31 October 2011), para. 244 based on *S.D. Myers, Inc. v. Government of Canada*, UNCITRAL, Award, para. 282.

already possess. Those manufacturers that cannot absorb the financial impact may even be driven out of business completely. The effect of the regulatory measure taken for public interest is not aimed at affecting the investments and the effect of the measure would be different for each investor. In contrast, the State decides to take away the land on which one car manufacturer is based. Or, the State wants to promote local manufacturers and to benefit them changes manufacturing standards and as expected investors are driven out of business. These would be instances of expropriatory measures.

Another way of looking at the distinction between regulatory and expropriatory measures is that several governmental actions affect all private entities, including foreign investors. For example, taxation laws are changed every year and impact private entities. If the distinction between a regulatory measure and an expropriatory measure is not maintained it will become impossible to run the affairs of the State. A taxation measure of the State by itself does not constitute an expropriatory measure, unless it has the features of an expropriatory measure. The position was summarized by Brownlie in the following words:

> State measures, prima facie a lawful exercise of powers of government, may affect foreign interests considerably without amounting to expropriation. Thus foreign assets and their use may be subjected to taxation, trade restrictions involving licenses and quotas, or measures of devaluation. While special facts may alter cases, in principle such measures are not unlawful and do not constitute expropriation.[33]

An expropriatory measure may be legal or illegal. It would be legal if it meets the criteria set out in the expropriation standard in the IIA and if they are not met then it is illegal.[34] In either situation State has to pay compensation. A regulatory measure does not attract the responsibility to compensate.

After having clarified the conceptual difference between a regulatory and expropriatory measure, the following sections assess the practical methods employed to distinguish the two. Initially in investment arbitration cases, there was a tendency amongst some tribunals to rely on the sole effects doctrine,

---

33 Ian Brownlie, *Principles of Public International Law*, 4th ed., Oxford, Clarendon Press, 1990, p. 532.

34 *Ioannis Kardassopoulos v The Republic of Georgia*, ICSID Case Nos. ARB/05/18 and ARB/07/15, Award (3 March 2010), para. 387; Ursula Kriebaum, Christoph Schreuer, Rudolf Dolzer, *Principles of International Investment Law* (3rd edn: Oxford University Press, 2022), p. 183.

primarily based on the cases decided by the Iran-US Claims Tribunal. The PCIJ, since early on had taken a view that the nature of the measure is to be assessed to decide whether the measure is expropriatory. It was inappropriate to look solely at the effect of the measure. The evolution and application of the two approaches is disused below.

2 The Sole Effects Doctrine

According to the sole effects doctrine, there is expropriation once the enjoyment of property is interfered. The government's intention is less important than the effect of the measures on the property of the investor.[35] States are said to have regulatory freedom but if it causes "irreversible and permanent" loss, State is responsible to compensate.[36]

The sole effects doctrine was propounded by Christie based on his interpretation of the *Norwegian Claims* and *Certain German Interests in Polish Upper Silesia* cases.[37] He used these cases to argue that the intention or reasons behind the measure are irrelevant. Once there is loss of property, the inevitable conclusion is that the property was expropriated. Thus, the effect of the action of the government on the property is the sole decisive factor.[38]

Neither of the cases on which Christie relied were cases of indirect expropriation, regulatory freedom or the relationship between indirect expropriation and regulatory freedom. These were cases of direct expropriation and the presence of an expropriatory measure was not in dispute.

The *Norwegian Shipowners* case related to the requisitioning order of the President of the United States directing expropriation of contracts for building or purchase of ships or material as a part of the war effort. The two principal questions decided in the case were whether "in fact" the requisitioning order extended to contractual rights and was there a failure on the part of the United States to pay compensation for the contractual rights. The Tribunal found that the United States, "seemed to have forgotten that it had assumed certain contractual obligations", for which the Tribunal ordered payment of

35 *Técnicas Medioambientales Tecmed, S.A. v. The United Mexican States*, ICSID Case No. ARB (AF)/00/2, para. 116.

36 *BG Group Plc. v. Republic of Argentina*, UNCITRAL, Award (24 December 2007), para. 268.

37 G.C. Christie, "What Constitutes A Taking of Property Under International Law," *British Yearbook of International Law* 38 (1962): 307.

38 G.C. Christie, "What Constitutes A Taking of Property Under International Law," *British Yearbook of International Law* 38 (1962): 307, 311.

compensation.[39] The tribunal never made any substantive determination on the 'intention' behind the measure since the Tribunal specifically noted – as was agreed by the United States – that there was an intention to requisition and therefore there was a responsibility to pay compensation.[40] The focus of the award was on the assessment of evidence to see which properties were factually covered by the requisitioning order.[41] Moreover, the Tribunal applied the municipal law of United States since the requisitioning measure was in capacity of 'eminent domain'.[42]

Christie used the following sentence from the award "whatever the intentions may have been, the United States took, both in fact and in law, the contracts under which the ships in question were being or were to be constructed"[43] to conclude that the tribunal disregarded the intention behind the measure and only looked at the effect. In Christie's words:

> contract rights were held to have been expropriated by the action of States which disclaimed any intention to expropriate such rights.[44]

The reference to the irrelevance of 'intention' in the award was not in relation to the requisitioning order but whether the United States had the intention to pay for the requisitioned property rights. This is clear from the paragraph immediately preceding the conclusions, where the Tribunal said:

> The Corporation may have intended, up to October 6th 1917, to settle accounts with regard to these claims, namely so long as it was expected that the property of the claimants would be restored at the end of the war but it "seemed to have forgotten ..."[45]

---

39 *Norwegian Shipowner's Claims* (*Norway v United States of America*), Permanent Court of Arbitration, Award, (1922) I RIAA 307 (13 October 1922), 324–325.

40 *Norwegian Shipowner's Claims* (*Norway v United States of America*), Permanent Court of Arbitration, Award, (1922) I RIAA 307 (13 October 1922), 324.

41 *Norwegian Shipowner's Claims* (*Norway v United States of America*), Permanent Court of Arbitration, Award, (1922) I RIAA 307 (13 October 1922), 318.

42 *Norwegian Shipowner's Claims* (*Norway v United States of America*), Permanent Court of Arbitration, Award, (1922) I RIAA 307 (13 October 1922), 323–324.

43 *Norwegian Shipowner's Claims* (*Norway v United States of America*), Permanent Court of Arbitration, Award, (1922) I RIAA 307 (13 October 1922), 325.

44 G.C. Christie, "What Constitutes A Taking of Property Under International Law," *British Yearbook of International Law* 38 (1962): 307, 316.

45 *Norwegian Shipowner's Claims* (*Norway v United States of America*), Permanent Court of Arbitration, Award, (1922) I RIAA 307 (13 October 1922), 324.

The factual conclusion of the tribunal that the United States extended its requisitioning measure to contractual rights and did not pay compensation was used to make the following legal claim by Christie:

> There are several well-known international cases in which it has been recognized that property rights may be so interfered with that it may be said that to all intents and purposes those property rights have been expropriated even though the State in question has not purported to expropriate.[46]

There was no occasion for the tribunal to comment on regulatory freedom or police powers and even the parties never argued issues of regulatory freedom or indirect expropriation. The *compromis* had already settled the question of law- the case was of expropriation and the scope of adjudication was limited to the extent of property rights expropriated. Scholars who have commented on the case throughout time have understood the decision to be on direct expropriation only.[47] Friedman had cautioned against mis-interpretation of the case even before Christie made his claims.[48] Unfortunately, scholarship in the field of investment law and investment tribunals relied upon the Charitie's assessment of these cases.

The situation of the second case *Certain German Interests in Polish Upper Silesia*, relied upon by Christie, was similar to the *Norwegian Ship Owners* case. The question before the PCIJ in the *Certain German Interests in Polish Upper Silesia* case was about the scope of expropriatory action of the Polish government. When the Polish government acquired a nitrate factory owned by the German Government the question was whether intangible

46 G.C. Christie, "What Constitutes A Taking of Property Under International Law," *British Yearbook of International Law* 38 (1962): 307, 316.

47 James W Garner, "An Arbitration Case Between Norway and the United States" *British Yearbook of International Law* 4 (1923–24): 159, 160; August Reinisch, "Expropriation" in *The Oxford Handbook of International Investment Law*, ed. Peter Muchlinski, Frederico Ortino and Christoph Schreuer (Oxford: Oxford University Press, 2008), p. 411–12.

48 "It is similarly necessary to deny any measure of authority to a second group of cases, frequently quoted by writers, ... the *compromise* or international agreement forming the basis of such a decision had already settled the question of law. As the function of the arbitral tribunal set up was limited, as far as legal questions were concerned, to the application of principles already laid down in the *compromis*, these decisions cannot be regarded as making any legal contribution towards the solution the problem under consideration." S Friedman, *Expropriation in International Law*, (London: Stevens & Sons Ltd, 1953), p. 69.

assets such as patents, licenses and contractual rights were also expropriated.[49] Poland argued that it was authorized to expropriate the assets of the German Government under the Treaty of Versailles but the PCIJ rejected the argument on the ground that only few States were given that authority and Poland was not one of them.[50] Yet again, Christie concluded that the Polish government did not 'purport' to expropriate intangible properties but those properties lost their value hence the loss of their value constituted expropriation and the intention to expropriate was irrelevant.[51] Contrary to Christie's claim, Poland admitted that its measures were expropriatory.[52] The question the PCIJ was deciding was the types of properties that were actually expropriated.[53] There was never a question of whether the measure was expropriatory or what was the intention behind the measures. The parts of the decision on which Christie relied were on the scope of the measure – that is whether factually the expropriatory measure was extended to intangible assets along with the tangle asset (in the facts of the case the factory).[54]

This time, Freidman was more caustic about superlative conclusions drawn from the *Certain German Interests in Polish Upper Silesia* case:

> Nevertheless, in view of the perfectly clear judgment of the Court, limiting itself to a consideration of a specific measure solely be reference to the conventional law of the parties, and of numerous statements in the pleadings placing the problem exclusively on this footing, to look for the hidden intentions of the Court by interpretation of some of its reasoning is to push legal analysis to a point where, departing from provisions sufficiently clear in themselves, it substitutes daring legal constructions which a regard for strict interpretation would not warrant.[55]

49 *Case Concerning Certain German Interests in Polish Upper Silesia* (*Germany v. Poland*) (1925) PCIJ Series A-No. 6, 9.

50 *Case Concerning Certain German Interests in Polish Upper Silesia* (*Germany v. Poland*) (1925) PCIJ Series A-No. 6, 27–31.

51 GC Christie, "What Constitutes A Taking of Property Under International Law," *British Yearbook of International Law* 38 (1962): 307, 311.

52 *Case Concerning Certain German Interests in Polish Upper Silesia* (*Germany v. Poland*) (1925) PCIJ Series A-No. 6, 19–25, 33.

53 *Case Concerning Certain German Interests in Polish Upper Silesia* (*Germany v. Poland*) (1925) PCIJ Series A-No. 6, 22.

54 August Reinisch, "Expropriation" in *The Oxford Handbook of International Investment Law*, ed. Peter Muchlinski, Frederico Ortino and Christoph Schreuer (Oxford: Oxford University Press, 2008), pp. 413–414.

55 S Friedman, *Expropriation in International Law*, (London: Stevens & Sons Ltd, 1953), p. 81.

The mischaracterization of these two decisions has led Friedman to say:

> In spite of the abundance of published material, perhaps even because of it, the question has remained obscure. Frequently invoked in the heat of legal controversy, the precedents selected have not always been analyzed with cold objectivity of the scientific method. Frequently it has been sought to prove too much, and precedents whose value is not considerable have been put forward as unquestionable authorities.[56]

Christie's conclusions came handy for the Iran-US Claims Tribunal (IUSCT).[57] The first articulation of the sole effects doctrine was done in *IIT Industries v Iran* in a separate opinion, appended to a judgment recording the settlement of the parties.[58] The separate opinion was given in the absence of a dispute and legal submissions of parties since there was already a settlement. This abstract separate opinion was referred in later decisions and came into currency.[59]

The IUSCT developed and applied the sole effects doctrine because its jurisdictional clause was quite broad. It extended to "expropriation or other measures affecting property rights".[60] The IUSCT treated this broad mandate to include all interferences with property rights, particularly the phrase 'other

---

56 S Friedman, *Expropriation in International Law*, (London: Stevens & Sons Ltd, 1953), p. 67.

57 See for a further analysis Aniruddha Rajput, "Problems with the Jurisprudence of the Iran–US Claims Tribunal on Indirect Expropriation" *ICSID Review – Foreign Investment Law Journal* 30 (2015): 589.

58 *ITT Industries Inc. v The Islamic Republic of Iran*, Award No. 47-156-2, (1983) 2 Iran-US CTR 348, 351–2 (Separate Opinion of Judge Aldrich) (26 May 1983), 348–349.

59 *Tippets, Abbett McCarthy, Stratton v. TAMS-AFFA Consulting Engineers of Iran*, Award No. 141-7-2, (1984) 6 Iran-US CTR 219 (22 June 1984), 225–26. See also *Phillips Petroleum Co. Iran v. Islamic Republic of Iran*, Award No. 425-39-2, reprinted in (1989) 21 Iran-U.S. C.T.R. 79, (29 June 1989) 115; *Starrett Housing Corp. v Government of Islamic Republic of Iran*, (Concurring Opinion of Holtzman) (1983) 4 Iran-US CTR 122, (19 December 1982) 162; *Harza Engineering Co. v Islamic Republic of Iran*, Award No. 19-98-2, (1982–3) 2 Iran-US CTR 499 (30 December 1982), 504; *Ataollah Golpira v Islamic Republic of Iran*, Award No. 32-211-2, (1983) 2 Iran-US CT 171 (29 March 1983), 177; *International Technical Products Corporation v Islamic Republic of Iran*, Final Award No. 196-302-3, (1985) 9 Iran-US CTR 206 (28 October 1985), 238–9; *Foremost Tehran Inc v Islamic Republic of Iran*, Award No. 220-37/231-1, (1987) 10 Iran-US CTR 228 (11 April 1968), 244; Above note 69 (*Tippets* Case), 225–6; *Phelps Dodge Corpn. v Islamic Republic of Iran*, Award No. 217-99-2, (1987) 10 Iran-US CTR 121 (19 March 1986), 130; *Constantine A. Gianoplus v Islamic Republic of Iran*, Award No. 237-314-1, (1986) 11 Iran-US CTR 217 (20 June 1986), 222; *Amco International Finance Corporation v Islamic Republic of Iran*, Partial Award No. 310-56-3, (1987)15 Iran-US CTR 189 (14 July 1987), 220–1.

60 Article II.1, Declaration of the Government of the Democratic and Popular Republic of Algeria Concerning the Settlement of Claims by the Government of the United States

measures affecting property rights'.[61] Explaining the thinking of the judges behind the expansive interpretation, Judge Aldrich who was a member of the IUSCT during the formative years of its jurisprudence on indirect expropriation admitted that "neither the terminology nor the intent of actions attributable to either Government would affect the [Iran-US Claims] Tribunal's jurisdiction to award compensation if the actions had adversely affected a claimant's property rights."[62]

The jurisdiction of the IUSCT did not contain a separate category of indirect expropriation. It included direct expropriation and the residual category: "other measures affecting property rights". The IUSCT did not distinguish between indirect expropriation and all other measures that affect property rights. Although the IUSCT dubbed them as indirect or *de facto* expropriations, the relevant cases were predominantly under the residual category.[63] Judge Brower explained in an opinion that there was no need to meet the rigours of indirect expropriation since the security account from which compensation was to be paid was created for the very purpose to compensate all losses.[64]

---

of America and the Government of the Islamic Republic of Iran (Claims Settlement Declaration), 19 January 1981, (1981–82) 1 Iran-US CTR 9.

61 *Kenneth P. Yeager v The Islamic Republic of Iran*, Award No. 324-10199-1, (1987) 17 Iran-US CTR 92 (2 November 1987), 99; *American International Group Inc. v The Islamic Republic of Iran*, Award No. 93-2-3, (1983) 4 Iran-US CTR 96 (19 December 1983), 101.

62 George Aldrich, *The Jurisprudence of the Iran-United States Claims Tribunal* (New York: Clarendon Press Oxford, 1996), p. 173.

63 Brunetti states that from approximately sixty awards rendered on the subject only few were based on any other measures affecting property and the bulk of awards are on indirect expropriation. While deciding cases on indirect expropriation, the Tribunals "have almost always applied customary international law". Maurizio Brunetti, "The Iran-United States Claims Tribunal, NAFTA Chapter 11, and the Doctrine of Indirect Expropriation" *Chicago Journal of International Law* 2 (2001): 203, 205; Veijo Heiskanen, "The Doctrine of Indirect Expropriation in Light of the Practice of the Iran-United States Claims Tribunal" *Journal of World Investment and Trade* 8 (2007): 215, 218–9.

64 *Eastman Kodak Company v The Government of Iran*, Award No. 329-227/12384-3, (Concurring and Dissenting Opinion of Judge Brower) 1987 (17) Iran-US Claims Tribunal 153 (11 November 1987), 173–4. There are various other instances where the Tribunal was lax due to the availability of the Security Account. See above *ITT Industries Inc. v The Islamic Republic of Iran*, Award No. 47-156-, (1983) 2 Iran-US CTR 348 (26 May 1983), 351–2 (Separate Opinion of Judge Aldrich), 349–52; *Tippets, Abbett McCarthy, Stratton v. TAMS-AFFA Consulting Engineers of Iran*, Award No. 141-7-2, (1984) 6 Iran-US CTR 219 (22 June 1984), 225–6; *Payne v. Iran*, Award No. 245-335-2 (8 Aug 1986), pp. 10–11; *Alfred L W Short v The Islamic Republic of Iran*, Award No. 312-11135-3, (1987) 16 Iran-US CTR 76 (14 July 1987), 78–9; *Arthur Young & Company Short v The Islamic Republic of Iran*, Award No. 338-484-1, (1987) 17 Iran-US CTR 245 (1 December 1987), 256; *Motorola Inc. v. Iranian National Airlines Corporation*, Award No. 374-481-3, Dissenting Opinion of Judge Brower,

The IUSCT preferred the term 'deprivation' over 'taking' because the latter is an outcome of an expropriatory measure where the government acquires private property, but deprivation is broad to include any effect on private property.[65] The cases although deciding expropriation claims were looking fundamentally at all deprivations of property, which required to look solely at the effect of the measure.

Early investment tribunals such as *Metaclad v Mexico* that adopted an expansive interpretation of indirect expropriation were influenced by the jurisprudence of the IUSCT.[66]

The *Techmed v Mexico* tribunal went to the extent to claim that the sole effects doctrine has become customary international law.[67] Even scholars supportive of the sole effects doctrine have not gone taken that extreme position.[68] The tribunal rejected the prospect of using regulatory measure on the grounds that the language of expropriation clauses did not exclude responsibility for losses arising out of regulatory freedom. There was no principle in the treaty to the effect that such measures were "*per se* excluded from the scope of the Agreement, even if they are beneficial to society as a whole-such as environment protection".[69] The tribunal was reluctant to accept regulatory freedom unless it was expressly mentioned in the treaty. Notably, the tribunal observed that regulatory freedom was a part of domestic law and could not be a justification for non-compliance with obligations under international law.[70] In contrast, the tribunal in *Apotex v United States* stated that there is

(1988) 19 Iran-US CTR 73, 85; *Phillips Petroleum Co. Iran v. Islamic Republic of Iran*, Award No. 425-39-2 (29 June 1989), reprinted in (1989) 21 Iran-U.S. C.T.R. 79, 115.

65 *Tippets, Abbett McCarthy, Stratton v. TAMS-AFFA Consulting Engineers of Iran*, Award No. 141-7-2, 22 June 1984, (1984) 6 Iran-US CTR 219, 225–26; *Phillips Petroleum Co. Iran v. Islamic Republic of Iran*, Award No. 425-39-2, reprinted in (1989) 21 Iran-U.S. C.T.R. 79 (29 June 1989), 115; *Starrett Housing Corp. v Government of Islamic Republic of Iran*, (Concurring Opinion of Holtzman) (1983) 4 Iran-US CTR 122 (19 December 1982), 162.

66 *Metalclad Corporation v. The United Mexican States*, Case No. ARB(AF)/97/1, Award (30 August 2000), para. 103; Aniruddha Rajput, *Regulatory Freedom and Indirect Expropriation in Investment Arbitration* (Kluwer International, 2018), pp. 61–66.

67 *Técnicas Medioambientales Tecmed, S.A. v. The United Mexican States*, ICSID Case No. ARB (AF)/00/2, para. 116.

68 Rudolph Dolzer, "Indirect Expropriations: New Developments?" *NYU Environmental Law Journal* 11 (2002): 64, 90–92.

69 *Técnicas Medioambientales Tecmed, S.A. v. The United Mexican States*, ICSID Case No. ARB (AF)/00/2, para. 121.

70 *Técnicas Medioambientales Tecmed, S.A. v. The United Mexican States*, ICSID Case No. ARB (AF)/00/2, para. 120. Further the Tribunal through footnotes 137–138 in the award relied on principles of State responsibility to support the position that municipal law is no defence for non-compliance with international obligations.

no customary international law that bars States from undertaking regulatory measures to address public interest.[71] It was discussed in the two preceding chapters that regulatory freedom is a part of customary international law. If the treaty provisions are a part of international rule of law, so are the rules of customary international law.

The sole effects doctrine is an outcome of case law of international courts and tribunals. It is not a rule of customary international law. Whereas regulatory freedom is a rule of customary international law. Judicial decisions are only subsidiary means for finding rules of customary international law but they by themselves do not constitute rules of customary international law. They have to give way to a normatively higher source of law in the form of customary international law.[72] Choosing between regulatory freedom and indirect expropriation is not a matter of "judicial discretion" as thought by the ad hoc Committee in *Patrick Mitchell v Congo*.[73] The consequence of the sole effects doctrine based upon the jurisprudence of the IUSCT is the expansion of the treaty obligations. Interpretation cannot serve as a process to expand the scope of treaty provisions.[74]

The distinction between a regulatory measure and an expropriatory measure if not appreciated, may result into confusion since both of them have an economic impact on the investor. If the economic impact is made the test to determine the presence of an expropriatory measure then all actions of State will constitute expropriation and regulation will become impossible. Therefore, the sole effects doctrine results into responsibility of States even for regulatory freedom. The crux of the controversy is distinguishing between indirect expropriation and regulatory freedom and the sole effects doctrine fails to address the matter satisfactorily. A competing and now a well settled approach in the decisions of international courts and tribunals, especially investment tribunals is to look at the nature of the measure.

---

71 *Apotex Holdings Inc. and Apotex Inc. v. United States of America*, ICSID Case No. ARB(AF)/12/1, Award (25 August 2014), para. 9.36.

72 Michael Akehurst, "The Hierarchy of the Sources of International Law" *British Yearbook of International Law* 47 (1975): 274, 280.

73 *Mr Patrick Mitchell v. Democratic Republic of the Congo*, Decision on the Application for Annulment of the Award, ICSID Case No. ARB/99/7 (1 November 2006), para. 54.

74 *Access to, or Anchorage in, the port of Danzig, of Polish War Vessels* (Advisory Opinion) (1931) PCIJ Series A/B No 43 (11 December 1931), 128, 144; Richard Gardiner, *Treaty Interpretation* (Oxford: Oxford University Press, 2008), pp. 144–7.

3 The Nature of the Measure

An analysis of the nature of the measure, to decide whether the measure is expropriatory was done prominently in the *Oscar Chinn* case.

In the *Oscar Chinn* case, United Kingdom brought proceedings on behalf of its national Oscar Chinn before the PCIJ against Belgium for the losses suffered due to the measures taken by Belgium in its colony Congo. The Belgian government operated a company in the field of fluvial transport on the river Congo and that company was in direct competition with Mr. Oscar Chinn's business. Being a government company, it was under an obligation to keep a permanent fleet in operation to meet the current and future needs of the colony at government approved rates and it had to remain in operation irrespective of whether it made losses.[75] During the severe depression of 1930–31, the Chamber of Commerce requested the Belgian government to intervene and lend assistance by reducing all costs of transport. The tariffs were substantially reduced and the government provided price support to the government company. The company provided a separate account for the duration was maintained and the annual statement of account or quarterly balance sheet showed a deficit.[76] These measures were issued in public interest and the rigour in their application ensured transparency.[77]

Without the price support of the Government as was extended to the government company, Mr. Chinn was driven out of business entirely. He had to suspend his transportation, shipbuilding and repairing business. Six other companies including Mr. Chinn approached municipal courts alleging that the government had created a monopoly in favour of the government company; but all these actions failed, including the appeal.[78] The government had expressed willingness to support the private operators if they provided the requisite guarantees to refund the losses after they make profit again.[79] But Mr. Chinn was already out of business.

75 *The Oscar Chinn Case (Belgium v United Kingdom)*, (1934) PCIJ Series A/B 65 (12 December 1934), 66.

76 *The Oscar Chinn Case (Belgium v United Kingdom)*, (1934) PCIJ Series A/B 65 (12 December 1934), 71–74.

77 *The Oscar Chinn Case (Belgium v United Kingdom)*, (1934) PCIJ Series A/B 65 (12 December 1934), 74.

78 *The Oscar Chinn Case (Belgium v United Kingdom)*, (1934) PCIJ Series A/B 65 (12 December 1934), 75–76.

79 *The Oscar Chinn Case (Belgium v United Kingdom)*, (1934) PCIJ Series A/B 65 (12 December 1934), 75–76.

Espousing Mr. Chinn's claim, United Kingdom alleged that the measure adopted by the Belgium Government created a *de facto* monopoly:[80] a situation similar to indirect expropriation where a State creates situations that force an investor out of business. The emphasis of United Kingdom's argument was on the 'effect' of the measure. The PCIJ rejected this argument and applied a three prong test to decide if Belgium was responsible: "nature of the measure", "circumstances of the case" and the alleged "international obligations" breached.[81] On the nature of the measure, the Court found that the measure did not apply only to government-controlled Company but to all businesses operating in the region and the reimbursement was allowed based on compliance with certain conditions and without discrimination.[82] Considering the circumstances of the case, the Court held that the Belgium Government was the sole judge of the circumstances and necessity of the measure. The government was obliged to keep the transportation service running and the critical financial situation required the Government to intervene. The measures had to be taken because the entire Colony was exposed to the threat of a major financial disaster.[83] Lastly, rejecting the interpretation that a treaty for promising freedom of trade and perfect equality means that all losses suffered by foreign investors under that treaty have to be compensated, the Court held that under such treaties States do not guarantee success of each individual business.[84] These treaties provided extensive protections and commentators have observed that the treatment standards in IIAs as regressive as compared to those protections.[85] In every business risk of loss is unavoidable[86] and treaty obligations do not serve as an insulation from losses.[87] Even under general principles of international law and vested rights in particular, there can be no vested right to profit.

80 *The Oscar Chinn Case* (*Belgium v United Kingdom*), (1934) PCIJ Series A/B 65 (12 December 1934), 69.

81 *The Oscar Chinn Case* (*Belgium v United Kingdom*), (1934) PCIJ Series A/B 65 (12 December 1934), 77.

82 *The Oscar Chinn Case* (*Belgium v United Kingdom*), (1934) PCIJ Series A/B 65 (12 December 1934), 77–78.

83 *The Oscar Chinn Case* (*Belgium v United Kingdom*), (1934) PCIJ Series A/B 65 (12 December 1934), 78–79.

84 *The Oscar Chinn Case* (*Belgium v United Kingdom*), (1934) PCIJ Series A/B 65 (12 December 1934), 85.

85 R. Dolzer and M. Stevens, *Bilateral Investment Treaties* (Hague: Martinus Nijhoff Publishers, 1995) pp. 10–11.

86 R. Dolzer and M. Stevens, *Bilateral Investment Treaties* (Hague: Martinus Nijhoff Publishers, 1995) 88.

87 R. Dolzer and M. Stevens, *Bilateral Investment Treaties* (Hague: Martinus Nijhoff Publishers, 1995) 85.

The Court recognized that Mr. Chinn lost his business entirely but that was not sufficient to hold the Belgian Government responsible. Acknowledging the exigencies of businesses and commercial environment, the Court stated that:

> No enterprise – least of all a commercial or transport enterprise, the success of which is dependent on the fluctuating level of prices and rates – can escape from the chances and hazards resulting from general economic conditions. Some industries may be able to make large profits during a period of general prosperity, or else by taking advantage of a treaty of commerce or of an alteration in customs duties; but they are also exposed to the danger of ruin or extinction if circumstances change. Where this is the case, no vested rights are violated by the State.[88]

The Court focused on the "motive and aim of the action of the Belgian Government" to decide whether its actions breached "perfect commercial equality".[89] The government company and Mr. Chinn could not be compared because the former had greater burden.[90] Overall, the emphasis of the Court in the reasoning is on the nature of the measure and not on the effect of the measure.

Some of the IUSCT cases looked at the nature of the measure when they had to assess whether the measure in question was regulatory. Interestingly, despite the wide discretion to hold a host State responsible for all losses arising out of measures of the State, IUSCT analyzed the nature of the measure and found that the State was not responsible for losses suffered by private persons due to the exercise of regulatory freedom by the State.[91] Emphasizing on the importance of the assessment of nature of the measure to distinguish it from an expropriatory measure, particularly indirect expropriation Sax stated that:

> the question never turns upon an examination of the economic consequences of the government's action; these theories postulate a qualitative

88 R. Dolzer and M. Stevens, *Bilateral Investment Treaties* (Hague: Martinus Nijhoff Publishers, 1995) 88.

89 R. Dolzer and M. Stevens, *Bilateral Investment Treaties* (Hague: Martinus Nijhoff Publishers, 1995) 86.

90 R. Dolzer and M. Stevens, *Bilateral Investment Treaties* (Hague: Martinus Nijhoff Publishers, 1995) 87.

91 *Emanuel Too v Greater Modesto Insurance Associates* (1989) 23 Iran-USCTR 378, 387–389; *Sea-Land Service Inc. v Iran* (1986) 6 Iran-USCTR 149, 164–165; *Sedco Inc. v National Iranian Oil Company* (1985) 9 Iran-USCTR 248, 275; *Dames and Moore v Iran* (1983) 4 Iran-USCTR 212, 221–223.

> difference between the police power and a taking, not a mere difference of degree.[92]

The cases discussed in the next chapter show the evolution of the approach of investment tribunals towards regulatory freedom, particularly the transformation from reliance on the sole effects doctrine to the nature of the measure to distinguish regulatory freedom from expropriatory measures.

4 Evolution of Investment Arbitration Jurisprudence

In early cases regulatory freedom was rejected and were deemed to violate the indirect expropriation standard. The tribunal in *Pope & Talbot v Canada* stated that "a blanket exception for regulatory measures would create a gaping hole in international protection against expropriation."[93] The expropriation provision of the NAFTA was, as per the tribunal, sufficiently broad to cover "non-discriminatory regulation that might be said to fall within an exercise of a state's so-called police powers."[94] Similarly, in *Techmed v Mexico* the tribunal strongly rejected regulatory freedom by saying:

> we find no principle stating that regulatory administrative actions are *per se* excluded from the scope of the Agreement, even if they are beneficial to society as a whole – such as environmental protection –, particularly if the negative economic impact of such actions on the financial position of the investor is sufficient to neutralize in full the value, or economic or commercial use of its investment without receiving any compensation whatsoever.[95]

The other prominent instance of rejection of regulatory freedom was *Santa Elena v Costa Rica* where the tribunal declared:

---

92 Joseph L. Sax, "Takings and the Police Power" *Yale Law Journal* 74 (1964): 36, 39.

93 *Pope & Talbot Inc. v The Government of Canada*, Interim Award, UNCITRAL (26 June 2000), para. 99. The Tribunal based these observations on the Third American Restatement on Foreign Relations Law in footnote 72, where it wrongly stated that the Third American Restatement considered the effect of the measure to be the sole criteria.

94 *Pope & Talbot Inc. v The Government of Canada*, Interim Award, UNCITRAL (26 June 2000), para. 96.

95 *Técnicas Medioambientales Tecmed, S.A. v. The United Mexican States*, ICSID Case No. ARB (AF)/00/2, Award (29 May 2003), para. 121.

> Expropriatory environmental measures – no matter how laudable and beneficial to society as a whole – are, in this respect, similar to any other expropriatory measures that a State may take in order to implement its policies: where property is expropriated, even for environmental purposes, whether domestic or international, the State's obligation to pay compensation remains.[96]

It is worth noting that this was a case of direct expropriation hence these observations need to be understood in that limited context.[97] The tribunal referred the task before it as the one to determine the consequences of an 'expropriatory measure'.[98] Its role was limited to decide the amount of compensation. The presence of an expropriatory measure was admitted and a regulatory measure was not involved.[99]

Tribunals that have adopted the sole effects doctrine look at the impact of the measure rather that its nature. For them once there is a substantial harm there is indirect expropriation.[100] Effectively, the purpose for the measure becomes irrelevant and it is immaterial whether the measure is a regulatory measure in public interest. In *Metaclad v Mexico* through a hypothetical example, the tribunal explained that even if a measure is taken for environment protection such as the creation of an ecological reserve on the landfill site in dispute, the State would still be responsible because the measure had an economic impact on the investor and the measure would be invalid.[101]

---

96 *Compañía del Desarrollo de Santa Elena, S.A. v The Republic of Costa Rica*, Award, ICSID Case No. ARB/96/1 (17 February 2000), para. 72. Tribunals relying on this award: Above note 12 (*Techmed v Mexico*), para. 121; *Compañiá de Aguas del Aconquija S.A. and Vivendi Universal S.A. v Argentine Republic*, Award, ICSID Case No. ARB/97/3, para. 7.5.15.

97 *Compañía del Desarrollo de Santa Elena, S.A. v The Republic of Costa Rica*, Award, ICSID Case No. ARB/96/1 (17 February 2000), para. 71.

98 *Compañía del Desarrollo de Santa Elena, S.A. v The Republic of Costa Rica*, Award, ICSID Case No. ARB/96/1 (17 February 2000), para. 72.

99 *Compañía del Desarrollo de Santa Elena, S.A. v The Republic of Costa Rica*, Award, ICSID Case No. ARB/96/1 (17 February 2000), paras. 7, 19, 20, 23, 54, 67, 73, 74.

100 *Nykomb Synergetics Technology Holding AB, Stockholm v The Republic of Latvia*, Award, The Arbitration Institute of Stockholm Chamber of Commerce (16 December 2003), para. 4.3.1; *BG Group Plc. v. Republic of Argentina*, UNCITRAL, Award (24 December 2007), para. 268; *Técnicas Medioambientales Tecmed, S.A. v. The United Mexican States*, ICSID Case No. ARB (AF)/00/2, para. 115.

101 *Metalclad Corporation v. The United Mexican States*, Case No. ARB(AF)/97/1, Award (30 August 2000), para. 109. These observations were found to be "extremely broad" by the court (Supreme Court of British Columbia) enforcing the award. The United Mexican States v Metaclad Corporation Reasons for the Judgment of the Honourable Mr Justice Tysoe, The Supreme Court of British Columbia, (2001) BCSC 664, para. 99.

The approach of these early tribunals has not stood the test of time. Noting the shift in arbitral practice, the tribunal in *Philip Morris v Uruguay* stated that "a consistent trend in favor of differentiating the exercise of police powers from indirect expropriation emerged after 2000."[102]

Tribunals that fall in this 'consistent trend' category have distinguished regulatory freedom from indirect expropriation and upheld regulatory freedom. They have upheld regulatory freedom based on different arguments but all fundamentally looking at the nature of the measure. Tribunals have upheld measures that constitute regulatory freedom despite their prejudicial effect on the foreign investment because regulatory freedom is a part of customary international law.[103] Furthermore, the inclusion of the reference to regulatory freedom in expropriation clauses in IIAs is seen as an acknowledgement of its customary international law nature.[104] Thus it is improper to look solely at the effect of the measure.[105] Even if a legitimate regulatory measure has the effect of "eviscerating the investment" there is no responsibility.[106] The position is customary international law is clear that "the State's exercise of its sovereign power within the framework of its police power may cause economic damage to those subject to its powers as administrator without entitling them to any compensation whatsoever is undisputed."[107] Legitimate exercises of sovereign rights to sanction violations of the law in its territory do not qualify as compensable taking.[108] The functional reason to uphold regulatory freedom, apart

---

102 *Philip Morris Brands Sàrl, Philip Morris Products S.A. and Abal Hermanos S.A. v. Oriental Republic of Uruguay*, ICSID Case No. ARB/10/7, Award, 8 July 2016, para. 295.

103 *Methanex Corporation v United States of America*, Final Award of the Tribunal on Jurisdiction and Merits, (3 August 2005), Part IV-Chapter D, para 7; *Crompton (Chemtura) Corp. v. Government of Canada*, PCA Case No. 2008-01, Award (2 August 2010), para 287; *Glamis Gold, Ltd. v. The United States of America*, UNCITRAL, Award (8 June 2009), para. 356; *Saluka Investments BV v. The Czech Republic*, PCA Case No. 2001-04, paras. 255–264; *Azurix Corp. v. The Argentine Republic*, ICSID Case No. ARB/01/2, Award, (CLA-296), (14 July 2006) para. 311; *EDF (Services) Limited v. Romania*, ICSID Case No. ARB/05/13, Award, ("EDF") (8 Oct. 2009) para. 293; *Link-Trading v Moldova*, paras. 68–9, 72–73.

104 *Saluka Investments BV v. The Czech Republic*, PCA Case No. 2001-04, Partial Award (17 March 2006), paras 256–262.

105 *Marvin Roy Feldman Karpa v. United Mexican States*, ICSID Case No. ARB(AF)/99/1, para. 109–117.

106 *Saluka Investments BV v. The Czech Republic*, PCA Case No. 2001-04, Partial Award (17 March 2006), para. 276.

107 *Técnicas Medioambientales Tecmed, S.A. v. The United Mexican States*, ICSID Case No. ARB (AF)/00/2, para. 119.

108 *Quiborax S.A. and Non Metallic Minerals S.A. v. Plurinational State of Bolivia*, ICSID Case No. ARB/06/2, Award (16 September 2015), para. 89; *Bank Melli Iran and Bank Saderat Iran v. Kingdom of Bahrain*, PCA Case No. 2017-25, Final Award (09 November 2021), para. 632.

from its character as customary international law is that they are necessary to uphold public interest:

> The Tribunal notes that the ways in which governmental authorities may force a company out of business, or significantly reduce the economic benefits of its business, are many. In the past, confiscatory taxation, denial of access to infrastructure or necessary raw materials, imposition of unreasonable regulatory regimes, among others, have been considered to be expropriatory actions. At the same time, governments must be free to act in the broader public interest through protection of the environment, new or modified tax regimes, the granting or withdrawal of government subsidies, reductions or increases in tariff levels, imposition of zoning restrictions and the like. Reasonable governmental regulation of this type cannot be achieved if any business that is adversely affected may seek compensation, and it is safe to say that customary international law recognizes this.[109]

The determination of whether a State has acted in public interest would need an assessment of the nature of the measure.

The perception of a "gaping loophole" in investment protection by recognizing regulatory freedom is an outcome of the misimpression about the limitations imposed by investment treaties on States. Also, it is a misperception that regulatory freedom is unbridled and extremely wide to protect all types of State measures. Indirect expropriation is an outcome of "unreasonable interference".[110] It is not simply any interference. Therefore, the standards of arbitrary, discriminatory and unreasonable are taken account of in the test for determining a regulatory measure. A general regulation that is arbitrary, discriminatory, disproportionate or otherwise unfair would constitute an indirect expropriation.[111] As clarified in *Link-Trading v Moldova*, a State is responsible for abusively taking property and explained abusive exercise in the following words:

---

109 *Marvin Roy Feldman Karpa v. United Mexican States*, ICSID Case No. ARB(AF)/99/1, para. 103.

110 *El Paso Energy International Company v. The Argentine Republic*, ICSID Case No. ARB/03/15, Award, 31 October 2011, para. 242.

111 *El Paso Energy International Company v. The Argentine Republic*, ICSID Case No. ARB/03/15, Award, (31 October 2011), para. 241.

> Abuse arises where it is demonstrated that the State has acted unfairly or inequitably towards the investment, where it has adopted measures that are arbitrary or discriminatory in character or in their manner of implementation, or where the measure taken violate an obligation undertaken by the State in regard to the investment.[112]

Measures taken by a State in response to a state of emergency are perfectly within the regulatory freedom of the State for which there is no responsibility.[113] The rationale for protecting regulatory freedom is that a State has to take into account and balance several competing interests. It is not possible to "please every constituent and address every harm with each piece of legislation".[114]

Not all governmental regulations that make "it difficult or impossible for an investor to carry out a particular business ... makes it uneconomical to continue a particular business, is expropriation."[115] Certain measures, such as taxation are an integral part of regulatory freedom.[116] Every taxation measure results into financial loss and in the absence of specific commitment, a State cannot be held responsible for changes to the taxation regime.[117] There is a presumption of legality in relation to certain State due to their nature. Explaining the rationale for the presumption, the tribunal in *El Paso v Argentina* stated that:

> The tax policy of a country is a matter relating to the sovereign power of the State and its power to impose taxes on its territory. The Tribunal agrees that the State has a sovereign right to enact the tax measures it deems appropriate at any particular time. Every year, governments around the world propose the adoption of tax measures which constitute either new initiatives or amendments to the existing fiscal legislation. There is a presumption of validity in favour of legislative measures adopted by a

112 *Link-Trading Joint Stock Company v Department for Customs Control of Moldova*, Final Award, (18 April 2002), para. 64.

113 *Suez, Sociedad General de Aguas de Barcelona, S.A. and Vivendi Universal, S.A. v Argentine Republic*, Decision on Liability, ICSID Case No. ARB/03/19, (30 June 2010), para. 140.

114 *Glamis Gold, Ltd. v. The United States of America*, UNCITRAL, Award (8 June 2009), para. 804.

115 *Robert Azinia v United Mexican States*, Award (1 November 1999), paras. 14, 83; *Marvin Roy Feldman Karpa v. United Mexican States*, ICSID Case No. ARB(AF)/99/1, para. 112.

116 *Link-Trading Joint Stock Company v Department for Customs Control of Moldova*, Final Award, (18 April 2002), para. 83.

117 *EnCana Corporation v Republic of Ecuador*, Award, UNCITRAL Rules, (3 February 2006), para. 173.

> State, and it is up to those who challenge such measures to demonstrate their invalidity.[118]

Terming as "the most appropriate approach", the tribunal in *El Paso v Argentina* upheld regulatory freedom after extensive discussion since, according to the tribunal "as a matter of principle, a general regulation – whose object is not the taking of property as in the case of direct expropriation – does not amount to an indirect expropriation."[119] States do not incur responsibility for legitimate exercise of regulatory freedom because:

> Governments must be free to act in the broader public interest through protection of the environment, new or modified tax regimes, the granting or withdrawal of government subsidies, reductions or increases in tariff levels, imposition of zoning restrictions and the like.[120]

Equally State need to change laws from time to time:

> Governments, in their exercise of regulatory power, frequently change their laws and regulations in response to changing economic circumstances or changing political, economic or social considerations. Those changes may well make their activities less profitable or even uneconomic to continue.[121]

A peculiar position was taken by the tribunal in *Magyar v Hungary*. The tribunal firstly noted that "an unqualified exception from the duty of compensation for all regulatory measures would hardly be compatible with the language of non-expropriation provisions of investment treaties".[122] But then relying on *Saluka v Czech Republic* it concluded that there is no responsibility of the State to compensate for losses to the investor in two situation: "the exemption from compensation may apply to generally accepted measures of police powers that

118 *El Paso Energy International Company v. The Argentine Republic*, ICSID Case No. ARB/03/15, Award, 31 October 2011, para. 290.

119 *El Paso Energy International Company v. The Argentine Republic*, ICSID Case No. ARB/03/15, Award, 31 October 2011, para. 236.

120 *Marvin Roy Feldman Karpa v. United Mexican States*, ICSID Case No. ARB(AF)/99/1, para. 103.

121 *Marvin Roy Feldman Karpa v. United Mexican States*, ICSID Case No. ARB(AF)/99/1, para. 112.

122 *Magyar Farming Company Ltd, Kintyre Kft and Inicia Zrt v. Hungary*, ICSID Case No. ARB/17/27, Award, (13 November 2019), para. 298.

aim at enforcing existing regulations against the investor's own wrongdoings, such as criminal, tax and administrative sanctions, or revocation of licenses and concessions" and "regulatory measures aimed at abating threats that the investor's activities may pose to public health, environment or public order."[123] Strangely the tribunal then sought to narrow down the scope of regulatory freedom by limiting it to "measures such as the prohibition of harmful substances, tobacco plain packaging, or the imposition of emergency measures in times of political or economic crises."[124] For the tribunal, a State is free to change its policies but "in doing so it was required to respect vested rights. In other words, it is not immediately apparent why this policy change – which purportedly benefited Hungarian society as a whole – should have been carried out at the expense of the Claimants' vested rights."[125]

The tribunal sought to restrict regulatory freedom through the doctrine of vested rights. For the protection of vested rights in international law two requirements are necessary. First, the right should have accrued and secondly the rights shall be incapable of modification or termination.[126] A growing number of scholars take the position that the investors' rights originating in the treaty are not directly possessed by the investors.[127] They are derivate rights incapable of attaining the character of vested rights. If the rights does not exist there is no question of it accruing or losing it for that matter. Hence, international courts and tribunals, including most investment tribunals have not allowed vested rights to be raised to bar the exercise of regulatory freedom by a

---

123 *Magyar Farming Company Ltd, Kintyre Kft and Inicia Zrt v. Hungary*, ICSID Case No. ARB/17/27, Award, (13 November 2019), para. 365.

124 *Magyar Farming Company Ltd, Kintyre Kft and Inicia Zrt v. Hungary*, ICSID Case No. ARB/17/27, Award, (13 November 2019), para. 366.

125 *Magyar Farming Company Ltd, Kintyre Kft and Inicia Zrt v. Hungary*, ICSID Case No. ARB/17/27, Award, (13 November 2019), para. 367.

126 August Reinisch and Sara Mansour Fallah, "Post-Termination Responsibility of States? – The Impact of Amendment/Modification, Suspension and Termination of Investment Treaties on (Vested) Rights of Investors" ICSID Review – Foreign Investment Law Journal 37 (2022): 101, 115–118; Pierre A Lalive, *Doctrine of Acquired Rights' in Rights and Duties of Private Investors Abroad* (Mathew Bender, 1965), pp. 183–5.

127 August Reinisch and Sara Mansour Fallah, "Post-Termination Responsibility of States? – The Impact of Amendment/Modification, Suspension and Termination of Investment Treaties on (Vested) Rights of Investors" ICSID Review – Foreign Investment Law Journal 37 (2022): 101, 118; Zachary Douglas, "Hybrid Foundations of Investment Treaty Arbitration," *British Yearbook of International Law* 74, no. 1 (2003): 151,163; James Harrison, "The Life and Death of BITs: Legal Issues Concerning Survival Clauses and the Termination of Investment Treaties" JWIT 13 (2012): 928–50, 943.

State.[128] The PCIJ expressly rejected the possibility of vested rights in relation to protection of foreign investors because there is a commercial risk of losses in every commercial transaction. Otherwise the State will have to compensate for every loss which is neither practical not the goal.[129]

Apart from the emerging consensus on upholding regulatory freedom by distinguishing a regulatory measure from an expropriatory measure, the approach of majority of investment tribunals is that before the question of expropriation is looked into, there shall be neutralization of assets.[130] Mere interreference is not sufficient, the deprivation has to be of a significant degree.[131] The investor must establish that "at least one of the essential components of the property rights must have disappeared for an expropriation to have occurred".[132] The tribunal in *Telenor v Hungary* did not venture into the question of the nature of measure because it did not find the losses to meet the threshold of neutralization.[133] Even if it may appear that in some cases mere loss of value was treated to constitute indirect expropriation, the reasoning would show that

128 H. Seddigh, "What level of Host State Interference Amounts to a Taking under Contemporary International Law?" *Journal of World Investment*, 2, no. 4 (2001): 631–84 at 646.

129 *The Oscar Chinn Case* (Belgium v United Kingdom), (1934) PCIJ Series A/B 65 (12 December 1934), 88.

130 *CMS Gas Transmission Co. v Argentina*, ICSID Case No. ARB/01/8, para. 262; *Enron Creditors Recovery Corporation (formerly Enron Corporation) and Ponderosa Assets, L.P. v. Argentine Republic*, ICSID Case No. ARB/01/3, para. 245; Sempra, para. 285; Continental, para. 276; El Paso, paras. 246–48; *El Paso Energy International Company v. The Argentine Republic*, ICSID Case No. ARB/03/15, Award, 31 October 2011, para. 299.

131 *S.D. Myers, Inc. v Government of Canada*, UNCITRAL, (12 November 2000), para. 283; *CMS Gas Transmission Co. v Argentina*, ICSID Case No. ARB/01/8, paras. 262–264; *Marvin Roy Feldman Karpa v. United Mexican States*, ICSID Case No. ARB(AF)/99/1, para. 100; *Electrabel S.A. v. The Republic of Hungary*, ICSID Case No. ARB/07/19, paras. 6.53, 6.63; *Pope & Talbot Inc v. the Government of Canada*, NAFTA Case, UNCITRAL, Partial Award, (26 June 2000), paras. 99, 102; *Sempra Energy International v. Argentine Republic*, ICSID Case No. ARB/02/16, para. 285, *AES Summit Generation Limited and AES-Tisza Erömü Kft. v. Republic of Hungary (II)*, ICSID Case No. ARB/07/22, paras. 14.3.1 to 14.3.4; *Charanne and Construction Investments v. Spain*, SCC Case No. V 062/2012, Award (Unofficial English translation) (21 January 2016), para. 461.

132 *El Paso Energy International Company v. The Argentine Republic*, ICSID Case No. ARB/03/15, Award (31 October 2011), para. 245.

133 *Telenor Mobile Communications AS v. Republic of Hungary*, ICSID Case No. ARB/04/15, paras 65–66, 69–70.

it was in fact referring to the necessity of neutralization rather than mere loss of value.[134]

The legal position on the relationship between regulatory freedom and indirect expropriation (an expropriatory measure) was summarized by the tribunal in *El Paso v Argentina* in the following words: In sum, a general regulation is a lawful act rather than an expropriation if it is non-discriminatory, made for a public purpose and taken in conformity with due process. In other words, *in principle, general non-discriminatory regulatory measures, adopted in accordance with the rules of good faith and due process, do not entail a duty of compensation.*[135]

Therefore, it is necessary to look at the nature of the measure to distinguish between a regulatory measure and an expropriatory measure. This is particularly important in allegations of indirect expropriation. Because every loss does not constitute an expropriation – direct or indirect.

---

134 *Consortium R.F.C.C. v. Kingdom of Morocco*, ICSID Case No. ARB/00/6, Award (22 December 2003), para. 69; *El Paso Energy International Company v. The Argentine Republic*, ICSID Case No. ARB/03/15, Award (31 October 2011), para. 254.

135 *El Paso Energy International Company v. The Argentine Republic*, ICSID Case No. ARB/03/15, Award (31 October 2011), para. 240.

CHAPTER 5

Regulatory Freedom and the Fair and Equitable Treatment Standard

Fair and equitable treatment has been the most successfully invoked treatment standard in investment arbitrations. The attractive feature of the standard is that it does not impose precise obligations on States like other standards. The imprecision of the standard has been used by investment tribunals as an opportunity to add elements to it. The fair and equitable treatment is an autonomous standard. Moreover, it is non-contingent that is the standard of treatment expected to be given to the investor is not contingent on treatment of other investors, like non-discrimination clauses – particularly the MFN and NT.[1] All the characteristics of the fair and equitable treatment standard make it a flexible standard allowing sufficient manoeuvrability to a tribunal to review measures of a host State. Consequentially, if the fair and equitable standard is interpreted widely, the scope of regulatory freedom will accordingly reduce. Like the interpretation of indirect expropriation, the interpretation of fair and equitable treatment has evolved overtime. With the developments in its interpretation, there is a potential for regulatory freedom to exist alongside fair and equitable treatment standard whereby a State would be responsible for its breach while exercising regulatory freedom.

The major difference in the relationship between regulatory freedom and indirect expropriation on the one hand, and regulatory freedom and fair and equitable treatment on the other is that for the former once the threshold of neutralization of assets is met, the focus is entirely on the nature of the measure. In the case of latter there could be two approaches. First, to apply the elements of fair and equitable treatment to the impugned measure and see if the measure is incompatible with one of the elements of the fair and equitable treatment. Second, check if a measure satisfies the requirements of regulatory freedom under customary international law. If it does then the measure is valid and there is no need to check if the measure has breached any of the elements of fair and equitable treatment. In *Philip Morris v Uruguay* the tribunal ventured into a discussion on the elements of regulatory freedom in relation to indirect expropriation but in relation to the fair and equitable treatment, the

1 *Total S.A. v. The Argentine Republic*, ICSID Case No. ARB/04/01, Decision on Liability (27 December 2010), para. 106.

 | DOI:10.1163/9789004759831_006

tribunal check whether the expectations of the investor could be termed legitimate in light of the nature of the sector and the prospect of regulations.[2] Tribunals have not been consistent with their approach, and is discussed in the following paragraphs.

Due to the flexible approach of tribunals towards the fair and equitable treatment it is difficult to state in abstract, the range of State actions that may breach the fair and equitable treatment standard.[3] The breach of the standard would be normally decided on the facts and circumstances of each case.[4] In the words of the tribunal in *Saluka v Czech Republic*, the determination of the legal meaning of fair and equitable treatment is "a matter of appreciation by the Tribunal in light of all relevant circumstances."[5] At the general, or so to say abstract level, as a matter of principle, a tribunal will take into account regulatory freedom. The fair and equitable treatment encompasses reasonableness and proportionality and ensures that "the foreign investor is not unjustly treated, with due regard to all surrounding circumstances."[6] One such 'relevant' or 'surrounding' circumstance is the public interest at stake and regulatory freedom exercised by States is to protect that public interest. The prospect of taking account of regulatory freedom and public interest while interpreting fair and equitable treatment is strengthened from the fact that the "interpretation of fair and equitable treatment standard in light of the object and purpose of the BIT may not exclusively rely on the interests of foreign investors."[7] Therefore, at the general level, regulatory freedom cannot be excluded. But the more complex question is how and to what extent the elements of the fair and equitable treatment standard affect regulatory freedom.

2 *Crompton (Chemtura) Corp. v. Government of Canada*, PCA Case No. 2008-01, Award (2 August 2010), para. 123.

3 *Total S.A. v. The Argentine Republic*, ICSID Case No. ARB/04/01, Decision on Liability, (27 December 2010), para. 107 quoting C. Schreuer, *Fair and Equitable Treatment in Arbitral Practice*, J. World Trade 6(2005/3): 357, 365.

4 *Total S.A. v. The Argentine Republic*, ICSID Case No. ARB/04/01, Decision on Liability, 27 December 2010, para. 109; *Mondev International Ltd. v. United States of America*, ICSID Case No. ARB(AF)/99/2 (11 October 2002), para. 118; see also *Waste Management Inc. v United Mexican States*, Award, ICSID Case No. ARB(AF)/00/3 (30 April 2004) and MTD Equity Sdn. Bhd. and *MTD Chile S.A. v. Republic of Chile*, ICSID Case No. ARB/01/7 (25 May 2004), paras 72–75.

5 *Saluka Investments B.V. v. The Czech Republic*, UNCITRAL, Partial Award (17 March 2006), para. 285.

6 *El Paso Energy International Company v. The Argentine Republic*, ICSID Case No. ARB/03/15, Award (31 October 2011), para. 373.

7 *El Paso Energy International Company v. The Argentine Republic*, ICSID Case No. ARB/03/15, Award (31 October 2011), para. 358.

The elements developed by arbitral tribunals while interpreting the fair and equitable treatment guide and control its application in specific situations.[8] From these elements legitimate expectations, stability of the legal framework, international minimum standard and arbitrary and unreasonable conduct interact closely and affect the application of regulatory freedom. The relationship with the impact of each of those on regulatory freedom is discussed in the following sections.

1 Legitimate Expectations

The fair and equitable treatment standard is "closely tied to the notion of legitimate expectations which is the dominant element of that standard."[9] Legitimate expectations requires that "the basic expectations that were taken into account by the foreign investor to make the investment" shall not be defeated by the host State through its actions or inactions.[10] Legitimate expectations "is an objective concept, that it is the result of a balancing of interests and rights, and that it varies according to the context."[11] Regulatory freedom is an important part of the context to decide the presence of and legitimacy of the expectations. Three factors for the assessment of legitimate expectations have been identified and these elements can constitute the basis to assess the relationship between regulatory freedom and legitimate expectations. *First*, "legitimate expectations cannot be solely the subjective expectations of the investor". *Second*, they "have to correspond to the objective expectations than can be deduced from the circumstances". *Third*, this can occur "with due regard to the rights of the State". Thus, "a balance should be established between the legitimate expectation of the foreign investor to make a fair return on its investment and the right of the host State to regulate its economy in the public interest."[12]

8 Rudolf Dolzer and Christoph Schreuer, *Principles of International Investment Law* (2nd edn: Oxford University Press, 2012), p. 133.

9 *Saluka Investments BV v. The Czech Republic*, PCA Case No. 2001-04, Partial Award (17 March 2006), para. 302 (footnote excluded).

10 *Técnicas Medioambientales Tecmed, S.A. v. The United Mexican States*, ICSID Case No. ARB (AF)/00/2, para. 154; *Saluka Investments B.V. v. The Czech Republic*, UNCITRAL, Partial Award (17 March 2006), para. 302.

11 *El Paso Energy International Company v. The Argentine Republic*, ICSID Case No. ARB/03/15, Award (31 October 2011), para. 356.

12 *El Paso Energy International Company v. The Argentine Republic*, ICSID Case No. ARB/03/15, Award, (31 October 2011), para. 358. Also see Moshe Hirsch, "Between Fair and Equitable

The reasonableness and appropriateness of the expectations is one of the tests to decide the legitimacy of expectations. The reasonableness and appropriateness of the expectations is a way to ensure that the expectations of the investor are not subjective.[13] The problem with subjective expectations is that it is impossible to meet them. They are like a moving target. An expectations will not be legitimate if it is unilateral. An expectations has to be based on "parameters such as business risk or industry's regular patterns."[14] Although ultimately they are the expectations of the investor with some subjective element involved, "the test of whether such an expectation can give rise to a successful claim at international law is an objective one."[15] What the investor believed to be its understanding and formed the basis of its expectations has to be based on its dealing with the government officials. It is therefore not enough that the investor sincerely held an expectation, but "the expectation must be reasonable and the Tribunal must make the determination of reasonableness in all of the circumstances." On the other hand, "[i]f the expectation was unreasonable (for example, ill-informed or overly optimistic), it matters not that the investor held it and it will not form the basis for a successful claim."[16] This is particularly important when it comes to the freedom of host States to exercise regulatory freedom. The recent trend in investment arbitration takes the view that "the requirements of legitimate expectations and legal stability as manifested in the FET standard do not affect the State's right to exercise its sovereign authority to legislate and to adapt its legal system to changing circumstances."[17] It would not be legitimate to expect a general stabilization of the legal framework.[18] That is the State cannot exercise its regulatory freedom because of expectations of the investor. Such an expectation would be misplaced. Moreover, it would not be merely unfair and inequitable to consider only the expectations of the investor, it would also be impractical. As stated by the tribunal is *Saluka v Czech Republic*:

Treatment and Stabilization Clause: Stable Legal Environment and Regulatory Change in International Investment Law" Journal of World Investment and Trade 12 (2011): 783, 789–790, 805.

13 *International Thunderbird Gaming Corporation v. The United Mexican States*, UNCITRAL para. 147.

14 *LG&E Energy Corp., LG&E Capital Corp. and LG&E International Inc. v. Argentine Republic*, ICSID Case No. ARB/02/1, Decision on Liability, (3 October 2006), para. 130.

15 *Invesmart v. Czech Republic*, UNCITRAL, Award, (26 June 2009), para. 250.

16 *Invesmart v. Czech Republic*, UNCITRAL, Award, (26 June 2009), para. 251.

17 *Philip Morris Brand SARL, Philip Morris Products S.A. and Abal Hermanos S.A. v. Oriental Republic of Uruguay*, ICSID Case No. ARB/10/7, Award (8 July 2016), para. 422.

18 *Total S.A. v. The Argentine Republic*, ICSID Case No. ARB/04/01, Decision on Liability (27 December 2010), para. 120.

> This Tribunal would observe, however, that while it subscribes to the general thrust of these and similar statements, it may be that, if their terms were to be taken too literally, they would impose upon host States' obligations which would be inappropriate and unrealistic. Moreover, the scope of the Treaty's protection of foreign investment against unfair and inequitable treatment cannot exclusively be determined by foreign investors' subjective motivations and considerations. Their expectations, in order for them to be protected, must rise to the level of legitimacy and reasonableness in light of the circumstances.[19]

The fair and equitable treatment requires that "a weighing of the Claimant's legitimate and reasonable expectations on the one hand and the Respondent's legitimate regulatory interests on the other."[20] The legitimacy of expectations of the investor are to be determined while keeping in mind that "States are in charge of the general interest and, as such, enjoy a margin of appreciation in the field of economic regulations."[21] As a part of balancing the rights of investments under fair and equitable treatment and regulatory needs of States, tribunals have alerted that overly expansive interpretation of the fair and equitable treated will negate the "the sovereign power of the State to regulate its economy."[22] In *Philip Morris v Uruguay*, the tribunal assessed each measure in question by "taking into account all relevant circumstances, including the margin of appreciation enjoyed by national regulatory agencies when dealing with public policy determinations."[23] Thus, "the threshold of proof as to the legitimacy of any expectation is high and only measures taken in clear violation of the FET will be declared unlawful and entail the responsibility of the State."[24]

19 *Saluka Investments B.V. v. The Czech Republic*, UNCITRAL, Partial Award (17 March 2006), para. 304.

20 *Saluka Investments B.V. v. The Czech Republic*, UNCITRAL, Partial Award (17 March 2006), para. 306.

21 *RREEF Infrastructure (G.P.) Limited and RREEF Pan-European Infrastructure Two Lux S.à r.l. v. Kingdom of Spain*, ICSID Case No. ARB/13/30, Decision on Responsibility and on the Principles of Quantum 30 November 2018, para. 262.

22 *El Paso Energy International Company v. The Argentine Republic*, ICSID Case No. ARB/03/15, Award (31 October 2011), para. 340.

23 *Philip Morris Brand SARL, Philip Morris Products S.A. and Abal Hermanos S.A. v. Oriental Republic of Uruguay*, ICSID Case No. ARB/10/7, Award (8 July 2016), para. 388.

24 *RREEF Infrastructure (G.P.) Limited and RREEF Pan-European Infrastructure Two Lux S.à r.l. v. Kingdom of Spain*, ICSID Case No. ARB/13/30, Decision on Responsibility and on the Principles of Quantum (30 November 2018), para. 262.

An expectation that the regulatory framework will not change at all is not reasonable because the circumstances in which the investment was made would never remain unchanged. As the circumstances change there would be a change in the legal framework to adjust, adapt and address those changes. Several factors contribute to those changes and they are not necessarily due to the actions or inactions of States. Therefore, to decide whether the "frustration of the foreign investor's expectations was justified and reasonable, the host State's legitimate right subsequently to regulate domestic matters in the public interest must be taken into consideration as well."[25] In some situations, the knowledge of the possibility of change in circumstances and consequential regulatory changes is put on the investor. Because an investor "must anticipate that the circumstances could change, and thus structure its investment in order to adapt it to the potential changes of legal environment."[26] The *telos* of FET does not indicate freezing regulatory freedom or placing absolute restrictions on changes to the regulatory freedom. Expectations cannot "be equivalent to freeze the regulatory framework".[27] Due to the nature of regulatory freedom and the extent of public interest involved, the assessment of frustration of the expectations, as expressed in *SD Myers v Canada*, "must be made in the light of the high measure of deference that international law generally extends to the right of domestic authorities to regulate matters within their own borders."[28]

The process of evaluation of State conduct involves "balancing the investor's right to be protected against *improper State conduct*, with other legally relevant interests and countervailing factors." [emphasis added] These factors include "the principle that legislation and regulation are dynamic, and that States enjoy a sovereign right to amend legislation and to adopt new regulation in the furtherance of public interest." However, the right to regulate "does not authorize States to act in an arbitrary or discriminatory manner, or to disguise measures targeted against a protected investor under the cloak of general legislation." Other countervailing factors include "the investor's duty to perform an appropriate pre-investment due diligence review and to show a proper conduct both before and during the investment."[29]

25 *Saluka Investments BV v. The Czech Republic*, PCA Case No. 2001-04, Partial Award (17 March 2006), para. 305.

26 *Parkerings-Compagniet AS v. Republic of Lithuania*, ICSID Case No. ARB/05/8, Award (11 September 2007), para. 333.

27 *Charanne and Construction Investments v. Spain*, SCC Case No. V 062/2012, Award (Unofficial English translation) (21 January 2016), para. 503.

28 *S. D. Myers, Inc. v Government of Canada*, UNCITRAL, Award, para. 263.

29 *Rusoro Mining Ltd. v. Bolivarian Republic of Venezuela*, ICSID Case No. ARB(AF)/12/5, Award (22 August 2016), para. 525.

It is noteworthy that the expectations can only be in relation to the legal and regulatory framework and not the state of the economy. Legitimate expectations would "necessarily vary with the surrounding circumstances".[30] A State cannot give any guarantee to foreigners concerning the health of the economy or make a promise to maintain the economic conditions prevailing at the time of the investment.[31]

The global economy is interconnected and regulations in one State can influence regulations in another State. Frequent changes to the regulatory framework around the world in a given sector may require regulatory changes in the host State thus limiting the predictability of the business and legal environment.[32] Rejecting the argument that the investor had legitimate expectations that their intellectual property rights would not be affected through regulatory changes, the tribunal in *Phillip Morris v Uruguay* referred to the practice of restricting intellectual property rights around the work and concluded that:

> Most countries, including Uruguay, place restrictions on the use of trademarks, for example in advertising. Particularly in an industry like tobacco, but also more generally, there must be a reasonable expectation of regulation such that no absolute right to use the trademarks can exist. Otherwise, "the mere fact of registering a trademark would guarantee the sale of any trademarked product, without regard to other considerations."[33]

Therefore the presence and contents of the legitimate expectations will depend on "the totality of business environment at the time of the investment",[34] particularly the general nature and characteristics of the economy.[35] In tran-

30 *El Paso Energy International Company v. The Argentine Republic*, ICSID Case No. ARB/03/15, Award (31 October 2011), para. 359.

31 *El Paso Energy International Company v. The Argentine Republic*, ICSID Case No. ARB/03/15, Award (31 October 2011), para. 365.

32 *Sergei Paushok, CJSC Golden East Company and CJSC Vostokneftegaz Company v. The Government of Mongolia*, UNCITRAL, Award on Jurisdiction and Liability (28 April 2011), para. 305.

33 *Philip Morris Brand SARL, Philip Morris Products S.A. and Abal Hermanos S.A. v. Oriental Republic of Uruguay*, ICSID Case No. ARB/10/7, Award (8 July 2016), para. 269 (footnote excluded).

34 *Saluka Investments BV v. The Czech Republic*, PCA Case No. 2001-04 (17 March 2006), para. 301.

35 *El Paso Energy International Company v. The Argentine Republic*, ICSID Case No. ARB/03/15, Award (31 October 2011), para. 360.

sitioning or developing economies an investor cannot expect same degree of stability of clarity as compared to that in a developed market economy. Regulations may be changed and there may be experiments with regulations. Foreign investors, in the words of the tribunal in *Paushok v Mongolia* are "acutely aware that significant modifications of taxation level represent a serious risk, especially when investing in a country at an early stage of economic and institutional development."[36]

The scope of legitimate expectations is decided based on the sector and the history of regulations in that sector.[37] For certain types of regulations and sectors by their very nature, there is a presumption that regulations in that field are bound to change, including major changes.[38] Environment protection is particularly one such area.[39] There are bound to be frequent changes in the field of environment protection. In *Techmed v Mexico*, the tribunal stated that the fair expectation based on the legal structure for the protection of the environment, it was evident that the powers of "supervision, control, prevention and punitive powers granted to the authorities in charge of managing such system, would be used for the purpose of assuring compliance with environmental protection, human health and ecological balance goals underlying such laws."[40] Tackling the effects of climate change would need extensive exercise of regulatory freedom. The Paris Agreement requires that the States undertake measures to transform and ultimately completely replace the existing sectors of the economy causing climate change. In such a situation even if at the time of investing the investors had an expectation of stability of the legal framework.

The nature of certain sectors is such that they are amenable to greater regulations and frequent regulatory changes. For example the tobacco industry is subject to heavy regulations and amenable to frequent changes. An investor is expected to be aware of the possibility of frequent and intrusive changes

36 *Sergei Paushok, CJSC Golden East Company and CJSC Vostokneftegaz Company v. The Government of Mongolia*, UNCITRAL, Award on Jurisdiction and Liability (28 April 2011), para. 302.

37 *El Paso Energy International Company v. The Argentine Republic*, ICSID Case No. ARB/03/15, Award (31 October 2011), para. 361.

38 *EnCana Corporation v Republic of Ecuador*, Award, UNCITRAL, (3 February 2006), para. 173; *El Paso Energy International Company v. The Argentine Republic*, ICSID Case No. ARB/03/15, Award (31 October 2011), para. 294.

39 *Methanex Corporation v United States of America*, Final Award of the Tribunal on Jurisdiction and Merits, (3 August 2005), Part IV-Chapter D, para 9.

40 *Técnicas Medioambientales Tecmed, S.A. v. The United Mexican States*, ICSID Case No. ARB (AF)/00/2, Award (29 May 2003), para. 157.

to the regulations.[41] The same applies to chemicals that may be treated hazardous in a State.[42] Public authorities have special roles and responsibilities when it comes to protecting public health and other important areas of public interest.[43] There can be no legitimate expectations within such sectors that States would not exercise or would only infrequently exercise regulatory freedom.[44] A tribunal must take into account all the circumstances, including the fact that certain agencies manage highly specialized domains involving scientific and public policy determinations.[45] Exchange control regulations fall in the category of the 'context' where States are known to exercise extensive regulatory freedom "in furtherance of their economic policy."[46] There is a preference towards margin of appreciation that allows greater freedom to States to regulate in certain sectors that are either prone to intense and changing regulations or involve serious public interest concerns.[47]

In situations of distress, it would not be legitimate for an investor to expect that a State would not exercise regulatory freedom. As noted by Professor Brownlie in his separate opinion in *CME v. Czech Republic*:

> It would be strange indeed, if the outcome of acceptance of a bilateral investment treaty took the form of liabilities 'likely to entail catastrophic repercussions for the livelihood and economic well-being of the population'.[48]

---

41 *Grand River Enterprises Six Nations, Ltd., et al. v. United States of America*, UNCITRAL, Award, (12 January 2011), paras. 144–5.

42 *Crompton (Chemtura) Corp. v. Government of Canada*, PCA Case No. 2008-01, Award (2 August 2010), paras. 6–8.

43 *Apotex Holdings Inc. and Apotex Inc. v. United States of America*, ICSID Case No. ARB(AF)/12/1, Award, (25 August 2014), para. 9.37.

44 *El Paso Energy International Company v. The Argentine Republic*, ICSID Case No. ARB/03/15, Award (31 October 2011), para. 400.

45 *Crompton (Chemtura) Corp. v. Government of Canada*, PCA Case No. 2008-01, Award (2 August 2010), para. 123; *Invesmart v. Czech Republic*, UNCITRAL, Award (26 June 2009), para. 254.

46 *Rusoro Mining Ltd. v. Bolivarian Republic of Venezuela*, ICSID Case No. ARB(AF)/12/5, Award (22 August 2016), para. 531.

47 *RREEF Infrastructure (G.P.) Limited and RREEF Pan-European Infrastructure Two Lux S.à r.l. v. Kingdom of Spain*, ICSID Case No. ARB/13/30, Decision on Responsibility and on the Principles of Quantum (30 November 2018), para. 262; *Philip Morris Brand SARL, Philip Morris Products S.A. and Abal Hermanos S.A. v. Oriental Republic of Uruguay*, ICSID Case No. ARB/10/7, Award (8 July 2016), para. 388.

48 *CME Czech Republic B.V. v. The Czech Republic*, Separate Opinion on the Issues at the Quantum Phases of CME v. Czech Republic by Ian Brownlie, C.B.E., Q.C., para. 78.

Due diligence by the investor can be decisive in the evaluation of expectations of the investor.[49] An investor has to undertake its own assessment of the legal structure and due diligence is a way to satisfy that requirement.[50] The importance of a due diligence will inform an investor about "the prospects of a change in the regulatory framework in light of the then prevailing or reasonably to be expected changes in the economic and social conditions of the host State."[51] Where the investor was alleging that its legitimate expectations were violated because the State did not provide State aid, the tribunal found that if the investor had done due diligence, it would have been informed of its prospects of obtaining State aid based on the domestic law and it could have even expanded the avenues of its prospects to obtain State aid.[52] Legitimate expectations are not to be lightly inferred.[53] Due diligence today has become a preliminary requirement since that is the basis to decide if the expectations of the investor were legitimate. The state of regulations and prospects and frequency of changes to regulations would be exposed through such an exercise. The freedom of States to regulate is protected through the knowledge of the investor and the scope of legitimate expectations is accordingly controlled.

An investor can argue the presence of legitimate expectations and the stability of the legal framework if there is a specific assurance from the host State.[54] If no specific assurances are given States retain wide regulatory freedom. In *Phillip Morris v Uruguay* the tribunal found that there was "nothing in the relevant legal materials to support a carve-out of trademarks from the legitimate realms of regulation." The national law of Uruguay, like other national laws of other countries following the Paris Convention system did not provide a

49 *Invesmart v. Czech Republic*, UNCITRAL, Award (26 June 2009), para. 254; *SunReserve Luxco Holdings S.À.R.L, SunReserve Luxco Holdings II S.À.R.L and SunReserve Luxco Holdings III S.À.R.L v. Italian Republic*, SCC Case No. V2016/32, Final Award (25 March 2020), paras. 711–4.

50 Anirudhha Rajput, "Due Diligence in International Investment Law: From the Law of Aliens to Responsible Investment," in Due Diligence in the International Legal Order, ed. Heike Krieger, Anne Peters, and Leonhard Kreuzer (Oxford Academic, December 3, 2020), 273–287.

51 *Philip Morris Brand SARL, Philip Morris Products S.A. and Abal Hermanos S.A. v. Oriental Republic of Uruguay*, ICSID Case No. ARB/10/7, Award (8 July 2016), para. 427.

52 *Invesmart v. Czech Republic*, UNCITRAL, Award, 26 June 2009, paras. 277, 281.

53 *RREEF Infrastructure (G.P.) Limited and RREEF Pan-European Infrastructure Two Lux S.à r.l. v. Kingdom of Spain*, ICSID Case No. ARB/13/30, Decision on Responsibility and on the Principles of Quantum (30 November 2018), para. 262.

54 *CMS Gas Transmission Co. v Argentina*, ICSID Case No. ARB/01/8, para. 27; *Total S.A. v. The Argentine Republic*, ICSID Case No. ARB/04/01, Decision on Liability (27 December 2010), para. 118.

"guarantee against regulation that impinges on the use of trademarks."[55] There was no obligation under international law that gave an absolute right to trade mark depriving a State to resort to regulatory measures hence the State possessed the regulatory power to regulate the cigarettes sector.[56]

As a general point, it is inconceivable to imagine that a State would fully abandon its regulatory freedom.[57] There can be no question of giving specific undertakings to generate legitimate expectations that the general regulatory framework would not change. It is not plausible to expect that the general regulatory regime applying to all and not limited to certain sector would not change.[58] It would be therefore be unreasonable to expect that the regulatory framework would not change. As per the tribunal in *El Paso v Argentina*:

> Under a FET clause, a foreign investor can expect that the rules will not be changed without justification of an economic, social or other nature. Conversely, it is unthinkable that a State could make a general commitment to all foreign investors never to change its legislation whatever the circumstances, and it would be unreasonable for an investor to rely on such a freeze.[59]

Likewise, in *Continental Casualty v Argentina*, the tribunal held that

> it would be unconscionable for a country to promise not to change its legislation as time and needs change, or even more to tie its hands by such a kind of stipulation in case a crisis of any type or origin arose. Such an implication as to stability in the BIT's Preamble would be contrary to an effective interpretation of the Treaty; reliance on such an implication by a foreign investor would be misplaced and, indeed, unreasonable.[60]

55 *Philip Morris Brand SARL, Philip Morris Products S.A. and Abal Hermanos S.A. v. Oriental Republic of Uruguay*, ICSID Case No. ARB/10/7, Award (8 July 2016), para. 270.

56 *Philip Morris Brand SARL, Philip Morris Products S.A. and Abal Hermanos S.A. v. Oriental Republic of Uruguay*, ICSID Case No. ARB/10/7, Award (8 July 2016), para. 271.

57 *Total S.A. v. The Argentine Republic*, ICSID Case No. ARB/04/01, Decision on Liability (27 December 2010), para. 115. (foot note excluded).

58 *Philip Morris Brand SARL, Philip Morris Products S.A. and Abal Hermanos S.A. v. Oriental Republic of Uruguay*, ICSID Case No. ARB/10/7, Award (8 July 2016), para. 426, 429.

59 *El Paso Energy International Company v. The Argentine Republic*, ICSID Case No. ARB/03/15, Award, (31 October 2011), para. 372.

60 Continental Casualty Company v. Argentine Republic, ICSID Case No. ARB/03/9, para. 258.

States can relinquish regulatory freedom in a certain sector and limit the freedom regarding certain types of regulations but that assurance has to be clearly established. This relinquishment will not be absolute if the circumstances change dramatically, such as an emergency. The nature of challenge will decide the degree of change: if the challenge is minor, it can be resolved through minor changes to regulations but if the challenges are major, major changes are to be expected.[61]

To generate legitimate expectations, a specific commitment will have to be made to the investor directly by the officials of the State. It cannot be based on "general statements in treaties or legislations which, because of their nature of general regulations, can evolve."[62] Most importantly, the investor should have relied on those assurances.[63] The assurances shall appear reliable on their face. The tribunal in *Total v Argentina* expressed the possibility of implied undertakings and that their reversal will violate fair and equitable treatment; but clarified that undertaking whether express or implied are not absolute and do not freeze the legal system of the host State.[64] Other tribunals have emphasized that regulatory freedom is necessary for a State to perform its functions as a sovereign State and its renunciation "is an extraordinary act that must emerge from an unequivocal commitment; more so when it faces a serious crisis."[65] A commitment to renounce regulatory freedom would "touch on core competences of the State, which it is inconceivable the State would implicitly renounce." Any guarantee of stability of its legal order or relinquishing its regulatory power "must be explicit and cannot be assumed through

61 *El Paso Energy International Company v. The Argentine Republic*, ICSID Case No. ARB/03/15, Award (31 October 2011), para. 363.

62 *El Paso Energy International Company v. The Argentine Republic*, ICSID Case No. ARB/03/15, Award, (31 October 2011), paras. 376–377.

63 *CMS Gas Transmission Co. v Argentina*, ICSID Case No. ARB/01/8, Partial Award, para. 611; *Técnicas Medioambientales Tecmed, S.A. v. The United Mexican States*, ICSID Case No. ARB (AF)/00/2, Award (29 May 2003), para. 154; *International Thunderbird Gaming Corporation v. The United Mexican States*, UNCITRAL, para. 147; *LG&E Energy Corp., LG&E Capital Corp. and LG&E International Inc. v. Argentine Republic*, ICSID Case No. ARB/02/1, para. 127; *El Paso Energy International Company v. The Argentine Republic*, ICSID Case No. ARB/03/15, Award, (31 October 2011), para. 376; *Plama Consortium Limited v. Republic of Bulgaria*, ICSID Case No. ARB/03/24, Award (27 August 2008), para. 176.

64 *Total S.A. v. The Argentine Republic*, ICSID Case No. ARB/04/01, Decision on Liability (27 December 2010), para. 120.

65 *RREEF Infrastructure (G.P.) Limited and RREEF Pan-European Infrastructure Two Lux S.à r.l. v. Kingdom of Spain*, ICSID Case No. ARB/13/30, Decision on Responsibility and on the Principles of Quantum, (30 November 2018), para. 244.

implicit declaration, diluted in general expressions."[66] Informal representations present difficulties hence "tribunals have increasingly insisted on clarity and the appropriate authority to give undertakings binding on the state."[67]

There can be no implied assurance not to alter the regulatory framework because States have entered into investment treaties. In the words of the tribunal in *Parkerrings v Lithuania*:

> It is each State's undeniable right and privilege to exercise its sovereign legislative power. A State has the right to enact, modify or cancel a law at its own discretion.[68]

Despite the presence of fair and equitable treatment a State maintains "its legitimate right to regulate, and this right should also be considered when assessing the compliance with the standard of fair and equitable treatment."[69] The laws in force are subject to reasonable change and there can be no legitimate expectation to the contrary.[70] If a promise is "lawfully granted" then any modification in the legal framework "should be done in a manner which is not disproportionate to the aim of the legislative amendment, and should have due regard to the reasonable reliance interests of recipients who may have committed substantial resources on the basis of the earlier regime."[71]

To sum up, the expectations have to be legitimate and it is not reasonable to expect that States would not change regulations or make new regulations to address changing situations. In certain sectors there would be a presumption of frequent regulatory exercises. An investor would need due diligence even before a credible argument of legitimate expectations could be advanced. It would be legitimate to expect that a State would exercise its regulatory freedom unless it is specifically abandoned.

---

66 *RREEF Infrastructure (G.P.) Limited and RREEF Pan-European Infrastructure Two Lux S.à r.l. v. Kingdom of Spain,* ICSID Case No. ARB/13/30, Decision on Responsibility and on the Principles of Quantum, (30 November 2018), para. 244.

67 *Blusun S.A., Jean-Pierre Lecorcier and Michael Stein v. Italian Republic,* ICSID Case No. ARB/14/3, Award, (27 December 2016), paras. 370.

68 *Parkerings-Compagniet AS v. Republic of Lithuania,* ICSID Case No. ARB/05/8, Award, (11 September 2007), para. 332.

69 *Plama Consortium Limited v. Republic of Bulgaria,* ICSID Case No. ARB/03/24, Award (27 August 2008), para. 176.

70 *Charanne and Construction Investments v. Spain,* SCC Case No. V 062/2012, Award (Unofficial English translation) (21 January 2016), para. 510.

71 *Blusun S.A., Jean-Pierre Lecorcier and Michael Stein v. Italian Republic,* ICSID Case No. ARB/14/3, Award, (27 December 2016), paras. 319, 372.

2 Stability of the Legal Framework

The stability of the legal framework was developed as one of the elements of fair and equitable treatment and legitimate expectations by investment tribunals. This element directly confronts regulatory freedom. The expectation of the stability of the legal framework reduces the freedom of the States to exercise regulatory freedom. Therefore this section focuses on the impact of stability of the legal framework on fair and equitable treatment.

The fair and equitable treatment has been interpreted by tribunals to serve as a tool to negate non-commercial risks. This has been achieved by treating the stability of the legal framework as a part of the legitimate expectations of the foreign investor and therefore a component of the fair and equitable treatment standard.[72] The relevance of the stability of the legal framework was explained in *Total v Argentina* in the following words:

> stability, predictability and consistency of legislation and regulation are important for investors in order to plan their investments, especially if their business plans extend over a number of years. Competent authorities of States entering into BITs in order to promote foreign investment in their economy should be aware of the importance for the investors that a legal environment favourable to the carrying out of their business activities be maintained.[73]

If the stability of the legal framework is treated as an absolute rule, host States will be responsible for every change to the regulatory framework. In

72 *LG&E Energy Corp., LG&E Capital Corp. and LG&E International Inc. v. Argentine Republic*, ICSID Case No. ARB/02/1, para. 125; *Occidental Exploration and Production Company v. Republic of Ecuador (I)*, LCIA Case No. UN3467, Final Award, paras 183–184; *CMS v Argentina*, Award, 12 May 2005, para 274–276; *LG&E Energy Corp., LG&E Capital Corp. and LG&E International Inc. v. Argentine Republic*, ICSID Case No. ARB/02/1, Decision on Liability (3 October 2006), para 124; *Sempra Energy International v. Argentine Republic*, ICSID Case No. ARB/02/16, Award (28 September 2007), para 300; *BG Group v Argentina*, Final Award (24 December 2007), para 307; *Bayındır İnşaat Turizm Ticaret ve Sanayi A.Ş. v. Islamic Republic of Pakistan (I)*, ICSID Case No. ARB/03/29, Decision on Jurisdiction, (14 November 2005), para 239; *Plama Consortium Limited v. Republic of Bulgaria*, ICSID Case No. ARB/03/24, Award (27 August 2008), para 173; *Merrill & Ring Forestry L.P. v. The Government of Canada*, ICSID Case No. UNCT/07/1, Award (31 March 2010), para 232; *Marion Unglaube v. Republic of Costa Rica*, ICSID Case No. ARB/08/1, Award (16 May 2012), para 248.

73 *Total S.A. v. Argentine Republic*, ICSID Case No. ARB/04/1, Decision on Liability (27 December 2010), para. 114.

other words there will be breach of the fair and equitable treatment standard with every exercise of regulatory freedom. In the literature, such as approach has been termed as 'hard' legal stability. Some early tribunals took the hard approach. For those tribunals, regulatory freedom is not simply diminished, but entirely vanished. The later tribunals have been careful and nuanced. Their approach has been termed as 'soft' approach, which is now the leading trend amongst tribunals.[74] The evolution of the soft approach in arbitration case law allows States to exercise regulatory freedom and do not treat that to affect the requirement of stability of the legal framework.[75] The exercise of regulatory freedom in these situations is unencumbered with the presence of the expectation of the stability of the legal framework. Increasing number of tribunals have started taking the view that the stability of the legal framework is not absolute.[76] If the stability of the legal framework is treated absolute, the fair and equitable treatment will operate like stabilization clauses in investment contracts.[77] IIAs do not contain or have an effect akin to stabilization clauses because States have not signed on to absolute standards through the

74 For a comprehensive analysis of the cases see Federico Ortino, "The Obligation of Regulatory Stability in the Fair and Equitable Treatment Standard: How Far Have We Come?" Journal of International Economic Law 21 (2018): 845, 849–850, 856–858; Yulia Levashova, *The Right of States to Regulate in International Investment Law: The Search for Balance Between Public Interest and Fair and Equitable Treatment*, (Kluwer Law International, 2019), pp. 117–133.

75 *Plama Consortium Limited v. Republic of Bulgaria*, ICSID Case No. ARB/03/24, Award (27 August 2008), para. 177.

76 *RREEF Infrastructure (G.P.) Limited and RREEF Pan-European Infrastructure Two Lux S.à r.l. v. Kingdom of Spain*, ICSID Case No. ARB/13/30, Decision on Responsibility and on the Principles of Quantum (30 November 2018), para. 315; *WCV Capital Ventures Cyprus Limited and Channel Crossings Limited v. The Czech Republic*, PCA Case No. 2016-12, Final Award (26 July 2023), para. 278.

77 *AES Summit Generation Limited and AES-Tisza Erömü Kft v. The Republic of Hungary*, ICSID Case No. ARB/07/22, Award (23 September 2010), paras. 9.3.29–9.3.30; *Stadtwerke Munchen GmbH, RWE Innogy GmbH, and Others v. Kingdom of Spain*, ICSID Case No. ARB/15/1, Award (2 December 2019), paras. 196–97; *Petroleum Servs. Ltd. v. Czech Republic*, UNCITRAL, Final Award (12 November 2010), para 285; *AES Corp. and Tau Power B.V. v. Republic of Kazakhstan*, ICSID Case No. ARB/10/16, Award (1 November 2013), para 401; *Feldman v. United Mexican States*, ICSID Case No. ARB(AF)/99/1, Award (16 December, 2002), para 103; *Saluka Investments BV v. The Czech Republic*, PCA Case No. 2001-04, Partial Award (17 March 2006), paras. 305–6; *Methanex Corporation v United States of America*, Final Award of the Tribunal on Jurisdiction and Merits, (3 August 2005), Part IV-Chapter D, para 7; *El Paso Energy International Company v. The Argentine Republic*, ICSID Case No. ARB/03/15, Award (31 October 2011), para 400.

fair and equitable treatment.[78] Investment treaties are "not good business insurance or a protection against a crisis."[79] Such expectations "would neither be legitimate nor reasonable."[80] Even when the matter is seen from the investor's perspective, giving the stabilization clause effect to the fair and equitable treatment "would go beyond what the investor can legitimately expect."[81] The tribunal in *EDF v Romania* made the position clear in the following words:

> The idea that legitimate expectations, and therefore FET, imply the stability of the legal and business framework, may not be correct if stated in an overly-broad and unqualified formulation. The FET might then mean the virtual freezing of the legal regulation of economic activities, in contrast with the State's normal regulatory power and the evolutionary character of economic life. Except where specific promises or representations are made by the State to the investor, the latter may not rely on a bilateral investment treaty as a kind of insurance policy against the risk of any changes in the host State's legal and economic framework. Such expectation would be neither legitimate nor reasonable.[82]

As was wisely noted by the tribunal in *El Paso v Argentina*: "it is inconceivable that any State would accept that, because it has entered into BITs, it can no longer modify pieces of legislation which might have a negative impact on foreign investors, in order to deal with modified economic conditions and must guarantee absolute *legal stability*."[83] Instead, legal stability is treated as a standard that "preserves the regulatory authority of the host state to make and

78 Christopher Campbell, "House of Cards: The Relevance of Legitimate Expectations under Fair and Equitable Treatment Provisions in Investment Treaty Law" *Journal of International Arbitration* 30, no. 4 (2013): 361, 379.

79 *Azurix Corp. v. The Argentine Republic*, ICSID Case No. ARB/01/2, Award, (CLA-296), (14 July 2006) para. 291.

80 *EDF (Services) Limited v. Republic of Romania*, ICSID Case No. ARB/05/13, Award (8 October 2009), para. 219; *Philip Morris Brand SARL, Philip Morris Products S.A. and Abal Hermanos S.A. v. Oriental Republic of Uruguay*, ICSID Case No. ARB/10/7, Award (8 July 2016), para. 424.

81 *Total S.A. v. The Argentine Republic*, ICSID Case No. ARB/04/01, Decision on Liability (27 December 2010) para. 120.

82 *EDF (Services) Limited v. Republic of Romania*, ICSID Case No. ARB/05/13, Award (8 October 2009), para. 217.

83 *El Paso Energy International Company v. The Argentine Republic*, ICSID Case No. ARB/03/15, Award (31 October 2011), para. 367.

change its laws and regulations to adapt to changing needs", of course "subject to respect for specific commitments made."[84]

The stability of the legal environment does not apply individually to each of the existing laws in the host State or any other applicable regional laws, such as the European Union (EU).[85] It applies to the entire legal system as it existed at the time of investment. A change to a certain law does not constitute breach of the fair and equitable treatment. The question then is: changes to what extent are allowed?

There are four approaches and responses. First, as is understandable, minor changes to the regulatory framework certainly do not breach the fair and equitable treatment standard.[86] The change has to be "radical or fundamental".[87] The fair and equitable treatment, as per the tribunal in *Eiser v Spain* protects "investors from a fundamental change to the regulatory regime in a manner that does not take account of the circumstances of existing investments made in reliance on the prior regime."[88]

The second approach is that stability of legal framework is not a part of fair and equitable treatment hence the question of the extent of change to the regulatory framework does not arise. The tribunals in this category, which are increasing in number do not follow the reasoning in *Eiser v Spain*. In *El Paso v Argentina*, the tribunal noted the impracticality of stability of the regulatory framework as an element of fair and equitable treatment. If stability of the legal framework was true, "legislation could never be changed: the mere enunciation of that proposition shows its irrelevance" and "if strictly applied, is not realistic, nor is it the BITs' purpose that States guarantee that the economic and legal conditions in which investments take place will remain unaltered *ad*

84 *Blusun S.A., Jean-Pierre Lecorcier and Michael Stein v. Italian Republic*, ICSID Case No. ARB/14/3, Final Award (27 December 2016), para. 319 (4).

85 *Total S.A. v. The Argentine Republic*, ICSID Case No. ARB/04/01, Decision on Liability (27 December 2010), para. 130.

86 *SunReserve Luxco Holdings S.À.R.L, SunReserve Luxco Holdings II S.À.R.L and SunReserve Luxco Holdings III S.À.R.L v. Italian Republic*, SCC Case No. V2016/32, Final Award (25 March 2020), para. 629.

87 *Foresight Luxembourg Solar 1 S.A.R.L, Foresight Luxembourg Solar 2 S.A.R.L., Greentech Energy Systems A/S et al. v. The Kingdom of Spain*, SCC Arbitration V (2015/150), Final Award, 359; *Novenergia II – Energy & Environment (SCA), SICAR v. Kingdom of Spain*, SCC Arb. 2015/063, Final Award (Feb. 15 2018), 654; *Eiser Infrastructure Ltd. and Energia Solar Luxembourg S.à.r.l. v. Kingdom of Spain*, ICSID Case No. ARB/13/36, Award (May 4 2017), 382.

88 *Eiser Infrastructure Limited and Energia Solar Luxembourg S.à r.l. v. Kingdom of Spain*, ICSID Case No. ARB/13/36, Award (4 May 2017), paras. 363, 382.

infinitum."[89] The tribunal rejected stability of the legal framework as an element of fair and equitable treatment in the following words:

> The tribunal declined to follow the cases whereby "fair and equitable treatment was viewed as implying the stability of the *legal* and *business framework*. Economic and legal life is by nature evolutionary."[90]

Similarly, in *Mobil v Canada*, the tribunal rejected the very concept of stability of the legal framework. It stated that the fair and equitable treatment "does not require a State to maintain a stable legal and business environment for investments" and does not aim at restraining changes governing investment "whether to a significant or modest extent". The fair and equitable treatment protects "only if those changes may be characterised as arbitrary or grossly unfair or discriminatory, or otherwise inconsistent with the customary international law standard." Due to the "complex domestic and international environment" there is nothing that prevents "a public authority from changing the regulatory environment to take account of new policies and needs, even if some of those changes may have far-reaching consequences and effects, and even if they impose significant additional burdens on an investor."[91]

Third, the nature of certain sectors is such that they are heavily regulated with frequent and radical changes to the regulatory framework. It would be unreasonable to expect that regulations would not radically change in such sectors.[92] For example, as noted by a tribunal, an investor entering oil and natural gas market cannot ignore "the real possibility of reasonable changes and amendments in the legal framework, made by the competent authorities within the limits of the powers conferred on them by the law."[93] Similar to the restriction on legitimate expectations due to environmental concerns, in the case of stability of the legal framework, where environmental concerns are involved and there is a wider participation of industry groups,

89 *El Paso Energy International Company v. The Argentine Republic*, ICSID Case No. ARB/03/15, Award (31 October 2011) para. 350.

90 *El Paso Energy International Company v. The Argentine Republic*, ICSID Case No. ARB/03/15, Award (31 October 2011), para. 352.

91 *Mobil Investments Canada Inc. and Murphy Oil Corporation v. Canada*, ICSID Case No. ARB(AF)/07/4, Decision on Liability and on Principles of Quantum (22 May 2012), para. 153.

92 *Philip Morris Products S.A. and Abal Hermanos S.A. v. Oriental Republic of Uruguay*, ICSID Case No. ARB/10/7, Award (8 July 2016), para. 429.

93 *El Paso Energy International Company v. The Argentine Republic*, ICSID Case No. ARB/03/15, Award (31 October 2011), para. 400.

non-governmental organisations, academic and other individuals seeking to pressurise the government to adhere to higher regulatory standards, the investor would be deemed to be aware that regulatory changes in such a sector would be frequent and drastic.[94]

Fourth, a radical change, for example, in taxation causing severe negative impact on the industry as a whole does not mean that the legislation is contrary to the investment treaty, as per the tribunal in *Paushok v Mongolia*. In the absence of a stabilization clause an investor should not be surprised with the tax increase because "such an event could not be considered as 'unpredictable'."[95] There shall be a clear agreement that the State has agreed not to revise its tax regime to show that the stability and predictability to constitute breach of fair and equitable treatment has taken place.[96]

If a tribunal takes the view from amongst the second to fourth approach, which seems to be the trend in arbitral jurisprudence, a host State can exercise regulatory freedom, even to radically alter the legal framework as it existed at the time of investment, as long as the changes are not arbitrary, discriminatory or unfair. A regulatory measure that satisfies the requirements under customary international law will certainly meet that threshold and will not constitute a breach of the fair and equitable treatment standard.

Overall, if a measure satisfies the requirements of regulatory freedom under customary international law it would not result into violation legitimate expectations and legal stability as manifestations of the fair and equitable treatment. In the words of the tribunal in *Philip Morris v Uruguay*:

> It is common ground in the decisions of more recent investment tribunals that the requirements of legitimate expectations and legal stability as manifestations of the FET standard do not affect the State's rights to exercise its sovereign authority to legislate and to adapt its legal system to changing circumstances.[97]

94 *Methanex Corporation v. United States of America*, UNCITRAL, Amended Statement of Defense of Respondent United States of America 2003, para 398, 407.

95 *Sergei Paushok, CJSC Golden East Company and CJSC Vostokneftegaz Company v. The Government of Mongolia*, UNCITRAL, Award on Jurisdiction and Liability (28 April 2011), para. 305.

96 *Sergei Paushok, CJSC Golden East Company and CJSC Vostokneftegaz Company v. The Government of Mongolia*, UNCITRAL, Award on Jurisdiction and Liability (28 April 2011), para. 305.

97 *Philip Morris Brand Sàrl (Switzerland), Philip Morris Products S.A. (Switzerland) and Abal Hermanos S.A. (Uruguay) v. Oriental Republic of Uruguay*, ICSID Case No. ARB/10/7, Award (8 July 2016) para. 422.

3 International Minimum Standard

It would be amiss not to discuss the effect of international minimum standard on regulatory freedom. Several IIAs have sought to control expansive interpretation of the fair and equitable treatment by tying it to the international minimum standard.[98] Despite its separate contents and acknowledgement as the proper standard to define the fair and equitable treatment standard, tribunals have insisted that the standard has evolved over time. That evolution is due to the interpretation of the fair and equitable treatment standard. The effect of that evolution on the regulatory freedom is the same that of the normal interpretation of fair and equitable treatment, as discussed in the preceding section. The focus of this sort section is on the international minimum standard as understood in customary international law and its relationship with regulatory freedom.

The threshold for establishing the violation of the international minimum standard is high. The international minimum standard is violated if:

> the conduct is arbitrary, grossly unfair, unjust or idiosyncratic, is discriminatory and exposes the claimant to sectional or racial prejudice, or involves a lack of due process leading to an outcome which offends judicial propriety – as might be the case with a manifest failure of natural justice in judicial proceedings or a complete lack of transparency and candour in an administrative process.[99]

It was stated *in Apotex v United States* that a regulatory measure satisfying the requirements of customary international law will certainly be way below this threshold. But if a purported regulatory measure falls below the threshold of the international minimum standard there is no margin of appreciation in favour of the State.[100] The requirement of *bona fide* (elaborated below) is

98 United States–Singapore Free Trade Agreement, 2004, art. 9.4, https://ustr.gov/trade-agreements/free-trade-agreements/singapore-fta/final-text. Exchange of Notes between the United Kingdom and Andean Countries, Year, accessed June 29 2024, https://www.gov.uk/government/publications/exchange-of-notes-between-the-uk-and-andean-countries; Hussein Haeri, "A Tale of Two Standards: 'Fair and Equitable Treatment' and the Minimum Standard in International Law," Arbitration International 27, no. 1 (March 1, 2011): 27–46, https://doi.org/10.1093/arbitration/27.1.27.

99 *Waste Management, Inc. v. United Mexican States ("Number 2")*, ICSID Case No. ARB(AF)/00/3, Award (30 April 2004), para. 98.

100 *Apotex Holdings Inc. and Apotex Inc. v. United States of America*, ICSID Case No. ARB(AF)/12/1, Award (25 August 2014), para. 9.37.

above the threshold of the international minimum standard. Also, the international minimum standard arises from customary international law. When a tribunal is applying the international minimum standard as a part of the fair and equitable treatment it has to also apply regulatory freedom as a part of customary international law.[101] Regulatory freedom can exist and be exercised alongside the international minimum standard and a host State will not be responsible for violation of the international minimum standard for exercise of regulatory freedom.[102]

4 Arbitrary or Unreasonable Conduct and Due Process

Either as a part of the fair and equitable treatment standard (including the international minimum standard) or an independent standard in an IIA, arbitrary or unreasonable conduct is a ground to hold a host State responsible for the breach of an IIA. The recurring theme in investment arbitration cases is that a State must not act unfairly, unreasonably or inequitably.[103]

An arbitrary or unreasonable measure is not based in reason or good faith but it is based on caprice, prejudice or personal preference.[104] An arbitrary conduct in international law is "a wilful disregard of due process of law, an act which shocks, or at least surprises, a sense of juridical propriety."[105] Black's Law Dictionary defines 'arbitrary' as "not governed by any fixed rules or standard", "performed without adequate determination of principle", "without cause based upon the law", or resulting from a "failure to exercise honest judgment".[106] Additionally, "arbitrary and capricious" is defined as the "characterization of a decision or action taken by an administrative agency … [as] wilful and unreasonable action without consideration or in disregard of facts

101 *Blusun S.A., Jean-Pierre Lecorcier and Michael Stein v. Italian Republic*, ICSID Case No. ARB/14/3, Award (27 December 2016), para. 319.

102 *WCV Capital Ventures Cyprus Limited and Channel Crossings Limited v. The Czech Republic*, PCA Case No. 2016-12, Final Award (26 July 2023), paras. 262–3.

103 *Parkerings-Compagniet AS v. Republic of Lithuania*, ICSID Case No. ARB/05/8, Award (11 September 2007), para. 332; *Técnicas Medioambientales Tecmed, S.A. v. The United Mexican States*, ICSID Case No. ARB (AF)/00/2, Award (29 May 2003), para. 154; *Rusoro Mining Ltd. v. Bolivarian Republic of Venezuela*, ICSID Case No. ARB(AF)/12/5, Award, (22 August 2016), para. 525.

104 *Lauder v Czech Republic*, UNCITRAL, paras. 221, 222, 232; *Plama Consortium Limited v. Republic of Bulgaria*, ICSID Case No. ARB/03/24, Award (27 August 2008), para. 184.

105 *Elettronica Sicula S.P.A. (ELSI) (United States of America v Italy)*, Judgment, [1989] ICJ Rep. 15 (20 July 1989), 42, para. 128.

106 Henry Campbell Black, *Black's Law Dictionary*, 6th ed. (1990), p. 104.

or law or without determining principle."[107] The measures of a State may harm economic interests of an investor but "if they have been adopted on the basis of objective criteria and cannot be considered irrational or arbitrary."[108] There is no arbitrariness if the measures were "based on a reasoned scheme to answer a major crisis and effectively had the desired result, which means that they cannot be considered as tainted by arbitrariness."[109]

Reasonableness, as a part of fair and equitable treatment requires that "the State's conduct bears a reasonable relationship to some rational policy, whereas the standard of "non-discrimination" requires the presence of rational justification for a differential treatment of a foreign investor."[110] The objective of the measure, based on the reasons that led to the adoption of the measure are the basis to decide if the measure was unreasonable. A measure based on good faith and proportionality is certainly not unreasonable.[111] Reasonableness is closely linked to fairness and covers a broad range of substantive and procedural requirements.[112] The concept of fairness means that the rights of the parties are respected and every step of the procedure follows the formal indication of the law.[113]

There is a relationship between arbitrary and reasonable. A measure that is supported by sound reasons is a reasonable decision therefore such a decision cannot be termed as arbitrary. There is no caprice or lack of candor in such decision-making processes. A measure would not attract responsibility if it is "not arbitrary but reasonable and consistent with the aim pursued."[114] There is a need of certain balance and the appropriate balance is that the host State does not act unfairly, unreasonably or inequitably, which in other words would

107 Henry Campbell Black, *Black's Law Dictionary*, 6th ed. (1990), p. 105.

108 *Charanne and Construction Investments v. Spain*, SCC Case No. V 062/2012, Award (Unofficial English translation) (21 January 2016), para. 534.

109 *El Paso Energy International Company v. The Argentine Republic*, ICSID Case No. ARB/03/15, Award (31 October 2011), para. 325.

110 *Saluka Investments BV v. The Czech Republic*, PCA Case No. 2001-04 (17 March 2006), para. 460; *S.D. Myers, Inc. v Government of Canada*, para. 98; *CMS Gas Transmission Co. v Argentina*, ICSID Case No. ARB/01/8, para. 290; *Impregilo S.p.A. v. Islamic Republic of Pakistan (II)*, ICSID Case No. ARB/03/3, paras. 264–270; MTD, para. 196.

111 *Total S.A. v. The Argentine Republic*, ICSID Case No. ARB/04/01, Decision on Liability (27 December 2010), para. 164.

112 Iona Tudor, *The Fair and Equitable Treatment Standard in the International Law of Foreign Investment* (Oxford University Press, 2008), pp. 126–127.

113 Iona Tudor, *The Fair and Equitable Treatment Standard in the International Law of Foreign Investment* (Oxford University Press, 2008), p. 126.

114 *El Paso Energy International Company v. The Argentine Republic*, ICSID Case No. ARB/03/15, Award (31 October 2011), para. 322.

mean that the host State acts in good faith. An integral element of regulatory freedom is good faith hence at the overarching level once a measure in good faith the measure should not result in violation of the fair and equitable treatment standard.[115]

Furthermore, the fair and equitable treatment entails "acts showing a wilful neglect of duty, an insufficiency of action falling far below international standards, or even subjective bad faith."[116] There are no restrictions on making changes to the regulatory framework, it is only the manner in which those changes are brought about. The threshold that certainly needs to be met to uphold a regulatory exercise is that "the host State must never disregard the principles of procedural propriety and due process and must grant the investor freedom from coercion or harassment by its own regulatory authorities."[117] Changes in regulations are not barred by fair and equitable treatment if the regulatory measure does not "exceed the exercise of the host State's normal regulatory power in the pursuance of a public interest".[118] The expectation is that the conduct of the State is in compliance with the "well-established fundamental standards as good faith, due process, and non-discrimination."[119] This expectation, which is enforceable as a part of fair and equitable treatment standard applies to during the life of the investment.[120] In *Saluka v Czech Republic* the tribunal had the following to say on the objective of fair and equitable treatment and its effect on regulatory freedom:

> A foreign investor protected by the Treaty may in any case properly expect that the [host State] implements its policies *bona fide* by conduct that is, as far as it affects the investors' investment, reasonably justifiable by public policies and that such conduct does not manifestly violate the requirements of consistency, transparency, even-handedness and non- discrimination. In particular, any differential treatment of a foreign

115 *Técnicas Medioambientales Tecmed, S.A. v. The United Mexican States*, ICSID Case No. ARB (AF)/00/2, Award (29 May 2003), para. 155.

116 *Alex Genin, Eastern Credit Limited, Inc. and A.S. Baltoil v. The Republic of Estonia*, ICSID Case No. ARB/99/2, para. 367.

117 *Saluka Investments BV v. The Czech Republic*, PCA Case No. 2001-04, Partial Award (17 March 2006), para. 308 (footnote excluded).

118 *Philip Morris Products S.A. and Abal Hermanos S.A. v. Oriental Republic of Uruguay*, ICSID Case No. ARB/10/7, Award (8 July 2016), para. 423 (foot note excluded).

119 *Saluka Investments BV v. The Czech Republic*, PCA Case No. 2001-04 (17 March 2006), para. 303.

120 *Saluka Investments BV v. The Czech Republic*, PCA Case No. 2001-04 (17 March 2006), para. 301.

> investor must not be based on unreasonable distinctions and demands, and must be justified by showing that it bears a reasonable relationship to rational policies not motivated by a preference for other investments over the foreign-owned investment.[121]

The tribunal in *Techmed v Mexico* stated that:

> The foreign investor expects the host State to act in a consistent manner, free from ambiguity and totally transparently in its relations with the foreign investor, so that it may know beforehand any and all rules and regulations that will govern its investments, as well as the goals of the relevant policies and administrative practices or directives, to be able to plan its investment and comply with such regulations.[122]

After setting out such high standards, in the same paragraph at the end, the tribunal concluded that

> Therefore, compliance by the host State with such pattern of conduct is closely related to the above-mentioned principle, to the actual chances of enforcing such principle, and to excluding the possibility that state action be characterized as arbitrary; i.e. as presenting insufficiencies that would be recognized "… by any reasonable and impartial man …"[123]

A coherent reading of the two parts of the sentence in *Techmed v Mexico* alerts that high standards of expectations from States are laudable but such an absolutist understanding may not be practical. The impracticality of excessively high standards was highlighted by the tribunal in *El Paso v Argentina* in the following words:

> Sometimes, the description of what FET implies looks like a *programme of good governance that no State in the world is capable of guaranteeing at all times.*[124]

---

121 *Saluka Investments BV v. The Czech Republic*, PCA Case No. 2001-04 (17 March 2006), para. 307.

122 *Técnicas Medioambientales Tecmed, S.A. v. The United Mexican States*, ICSID Case No. ARB (AF)/00/2, Award (29 May 2003), para. 154.

123 *Técnicas Medioambientales Tecmed, S.A. v. The United Mexican States*, ICSID Case No. ARB (AF)/00/2, Award (29 May 2003), para. 154.

124 *El Paso Energy International Company v. The Argentine Republic*, ICSID Case No. ARB/03/15, Award, 31 October 2011, para. 342.

Therefore, fair and equitable treatment does not freeze regulatory freedom. States retain regulatory freedom, provided they meet the requirements of regulatory freedom which are above the threshold of the obligations imposed under fair and equitable treatment. Once a measure satisfies the requirements under customary international law, it does not violate the fair and equitable treatment standard. The following chapter elaborates the elements of the regulatory freedom. It is only when a State can establish that these elements are met that a measure would not result into breach of treatment standards in IIAs.

CHAPTER 6

Elements of Regulatory Freedom

While regulatory freedom is essential and an integral part of existence and duties of a State, it is not absolute or limitless. Within customary international law, and as acknowledged by international courts and tribunals, including investment tribunals, a measure has to satisfy certain conditions in order to be treated as regulatory freedom. Only then will such a measure not result into violation of treatment standards. The synthesis of customary international law and the decisions of international courts and tribunals indicates that a measure has to be in good faith (*bona fide*), non-discriminatory and public interest. The tribunal in *Methanex v USA* also added due process.[1]

1 Good Faith (bona fide)

Bona fide or good faith is a pivotal element of regulatory freedom because it is often the decisive element and it influences the application of other elements of regulatory freedom. Good faith serves as a tipping point for distinguishing a regulatory freedom, whereby a State can adopt a measure that may cause harm to the foreign investor versus any other measure, for which a State is responsible to compensate for the harm caused. Regulatory freedom must be in good faith because "the deference to the State's regulatory powers cannot amount to condoning behaviors that are manifestly arbitrary, idiosyncratic, or that show a complete lack of candor in the conduction of the regulatory process."[2]

Good faith is described by the ICJ as "one of the basic principles governing the creation and performance of legal obligations".[3] The VCLT requires the parties to a treaty to act in good faith and an adjudicator to interpret the treaty in good faith.[4] In both situations the goal of good faith is to ensure that the treaty is complied with in both 'letter' and 'spirit'. Good faith has such an important role in treaty interpretation and adjudication because a treaty is

1 *Methanex Corporation v United States of America*, Final Award of the Tribunal on Jurisdiction and Merits, (3 August 2005), Part IV-Chapter D, para 16.

2 *TECO Guatemala Holdings, LLC v. Republic of Guatemala*, ICSID Case No. ARB/10/23, Award (19 December 2013), para. 492–3.

3 *Nuclear Tests, (Australia/New Zealand v France)* [1974] ICJ Reports 268, (20 December 1974) para. 49.

4 Vienna Convention on the Law of Treaties, 23 May 1969, 1155 U.N.T.S. 331, Article 26 and 31.

 | DOI:10.1163/9789004759831_007

limited to its subject matter and States are left with wide discretion on other matters. Treaties do not efface the discretion of States to exercise their sovereign authority to regulate domestic matters. But that sovereign authority if treated limitless, can serve as a tool to defeat treaty obligations. Good faith maintains the balance between the inherent right to regulate on the one hand and respect for treaty obligations. The relationship between discretion of a State vis-à-vis obligations under a treaty was explained by the Appellate Body of the WTO in the following words:

> The chapeau of Article XX is, in fact, but one expression of the principle of good faith. This principle, at once a general principle of law and a general principle of international law, controls the exercise of rights by states. One application of this general principle, the application widely known as the doctrine of *abus de droit*, prohibits the abusive exercise of a state's rights and enjoins that whenever the assertion of a right 'impinges on the field covered by [a] treaty obligation, it must be exercised bona fide, that is to say, reasonably'. An abusive exercise by a member of its own treaty right results in a breach of the treaty rights of the other members and, as well, a violation of the treaty obligation of the Member so acting.[5]

The PCIJ held in the *Certain German Interests* case that regulatory measures adopted in good faith do not violate treaty obligations.[6] In the absence of the restriction of good faith, discretion could be exercised abusively to defeat treaty obligations.[7] By regulating the conduct of the State outside treaty obligations, good faith ensures that States act reasonably and the actions performed outside the treaty framework are not conducted in a manner to defeat the treaty provisions.[8] To that extent good faith, in the words of the ICJ 'tapers' the sovereign discretion of States by requiring the States to exercise sovereign power reasonably.[9]

---

5 *United States- Import Prohibition of Certain Shrimp and Shrimp Products*, Report of the Panel, WT/DS58 (15 May 1998), para 158.

6 *Case Concerning Certain German Interests in Polish Upper Silesia* (*Germany v Poland*), Judgment, (1925) PCIJ Series A-No. 7 (25 May 1926), p. 30.

7 *Legal Consequences for States of the Continued Presence of South Africa in Namibia* (*South West Africa*) *notwithstanding Security Council Resolution 276* (*1970*), Advisory Opinion, [1971] ICJ Rep. 16 (21 June 1971), para 90.

8 *The North Atlantic Coast Fisheries Case* (*Great Britain v United States of America*), Award of the Tribunal, Permanent Court of Arbitration, (1961) XI RIAA 167 (7 September 1910), 189.

9 *Conditions of Admission of a State to Membership in the United Nations* (*Article 4 of the Charter*), Advisory Opinion, Individual Opinion by M. Alvarez, (1948) ICJ Reports 57

Good faith ensures that one of the parties does not gain an unfair or unjust advantage over another.[10] Equally, good faith requires that the regulatory freedom shall be genuinely used for the "pursuit of those interests which the right is destined to protect".[11] Therefore, if a State is exercising regulatory freedom in public interest, not to gain an unfair advantage over the foreign investors, then the regulatory measure would be consistent with the obligation to execute the treaty in good faith and does not violate the treaty.[12]

A change of policy aimed at stricter and swifter enforcement procedures, after a change in the political administration of a State does not constitute breach of treatment standards if the change in policy is made in good faith and not especially targeted or sought to discriminate against the investor.[13] If the aim of the measure is to defeat the investment and public interest is used as a disguise to harm the investment or the investor, such a measure would not be protected by regulatory freedom. The measure would be unlawful.[14] For example, measures aimed at indirectly ending the concession and forcing renegotiations are not legitimate regulatory exercises.[15] A "financially motivated and illegitimate regulatory expropriation by a regulator lacking in independence" would not be a regulatory exercise.[16]

The aim or goal of the measure is more important than subjective motives. Disregarding the motives, the tribunal in *AES v Hungary* found that the State was "principally motivated by the politics surrounding so-called luxury profits". Nevertheless the Tribunal found that it was a "perfectly valid and rational policy objective for a government to address luxury profits." This policy was not

(28 May 1948), 71; Bin Cheng, *General Principles of Law as Applied by International Courts and Tribunals* (London: Stevens and Sons, 1953), pp. 124–125.

10 Antony D'Amato, "Good Faith" Encyclopedia of Public International Law (1992): 599, 599.

11 Bin Cheng, *General Principles of Law as Applied by International Courts and Tribunals* (London: Stevens and Sons, 1953), pp. 125, 131–132.

12 *The North Atlantic Coast Fisheries Case* (*Great Britain v United States of America*), Award of the Tribunal, Permanent Court of Arbitration, (1961) XI RIAA 167 (7 September 1910), 189.

13 *Apotex Holdings Inc. and Apotex Inc. v. United States of America*, ICSID Case No. ARB(AF)/12/1, Award (25 August 2014), para. 8.75.

14 *B3 Croatian Courier Coöperatief U.A. v. Republic of Croatia*, ICSID Case No. ARB/15/5, Excerpts of Award (15 April 2019), para. 891; *Tethyan Copper Company Pty Limited v. Islamic Republic of Pakistan*, ICSID Case No. ARB/12/1, Decision on Jurisdiction and Liability (10 November 2017), para. 1329.

15 *Compañía de Aguas del Aconquija S.A. and Vivendi Universal S.A. v. Argentine Republic*, ICSID Case No. ARB/97/3, Award (20 August 2007), para. 7.5.22.

16 *Deutsche Bank AG v. Democratic Socialist Republic of Sri Lanka*, ICSID Case No. ARB/09/2, Award (31 October 2012), paras. 523–4.

seen as irrational, particularly since "so-called excessive profits may well give rise to legitimate reasons for governments to regulate or re-regulate."[17]

The presence or absence of good faith is to be proved through evidence and not presumed.[18] Good faith is determined based on evidence which can establish the intention behind the actions. This would involve assessing the material that formed the basis of the decision, circumstantial evidence based on words and actions of the officials of the State.[19] The *bona fides* of a State for resorting to a measure can be established based on the material that formed the basis of the measure. There must be contemporaneous evidence establishing the purpose for which the regulations were adopted.[20]

The ICJ has determined subjective intention behind the actions of a State by reviewing the circumstances under which the decision was taken and the manner in which that decision was executed.[21] Panels and the Appellate Body of the WTO have applied similar methodology for determining the subjective intention behind a measure.[22] Investment tribunals have used the material forming the basis of the decision to find if the regulation was *bona fide*. Explaining the methodology, the tribunal in *SD Myers v. Canada* stated the following:

17 *AES Summit Generation Limited and AES-Tisza Erömü Kft v. The Republic of Hungary*, ICSID Case No. ARB/07/22, Award, (23 September 2010), para. 10.3.34.

18 *Free Zones of Upper Savoy and the District of Gex* (France v Switzerland), Judgment, 1930 PCIJ Series A/B, No. 24 (6 December 1930) 12.

19 Andrei Mamolea, "Good Faith Review" in *Deference in International Courts and Tribunals: Standard of Review and Margin of Appreciation*, ed. Lukasz Gruszczynski and Wouter Wermer (Oxford: Oxford University Press, 2014), pp. 75–76, 85.

20 Resp. C-Mem., paragraph -368, *Nachingwea U.K. Limited, Ntaka Nickel Holdings Limited and Nachingwea Nickel Limited v. United Republic of Tanzania*, ICSID Case No. ARB/20/38, Award (14 July 2023), para. 240.

21 *Certain Questions of Mutual Assistance in Criminal Matters (Djibouti v. France)*, Judgment, [2008] ICJ Reports 177 (4 June 2008), para 140, 150–152; *Military and Paramilitary Activities in and against Nicaragua (Nicaragua v United States of America)*, Judgment, 1986 ICJ Reports 14 (27 June 1986), para 200, 234–6; *Armed Activities on the Territory of the Congo (Democratic Republic of the Congo v. Uganda)*, Judgment, [2005] ICJ Reports 168 (19 December 2005), paras 119, 143.

22 *Japan – Taxes on Alcoholic Beverages*, Appellate Body, WT/DS8/AB/R, WT/DS10/AB/R, WT/DS11/AB/R, (4 October 1996), paras 27–8; *Canada – Certain Measures Concerning Periodicals*, Appellate Body WT/DS31/AB/R, (30 July 1997), para 30; *Mexico – Tax Measures on Soft Drinks and Other Beverages*, Panel Report, WT/DS308/R (24 March 2006), paras 8.91–8.95; cf *United States – Certain Country of Origin Labeling (COOL) Requirements*, Appellate Body, WT/DS384/AB/R (23 July 2012), para 420; *Chile – Taxes on Alcoholic Beverages* WT/DS110/AB/R, Report of Appellate Body, (13 December 1999), para 74; Nicolas Diebold, *Non-Discrimination in International Trade in Services* (Cambridge: Cambridge University Press, 2010), p. 84.

> The intent of government is a complex and multifaceted matter. Government decisions are shaped by different politicians and officials with differing philosophies and perspectives. Each of the many persons involved in framing government policy may approach a problem from a variety of different policy objectives and may sometimes take into account partisan political factors or career concerns. The Tribunal can only characterize Canada's motivation or intent fairly by examining the record of the evidence as a whole.[23]

After considering various aspects and levels of the decision-making process, particularly: formulation to policy, bureaucratic process and debates in the Parliament, the tribunal found that the regulations were passed with the intention to protect Canadian industry to discriminate against foreign investors.[24]

Additionally, if a measure is tainted by intention to injure, fictitious exercise aimed at defeating treaty provisions, colourable exercise, regulations adopted solely for malicious purpose, and arbitrary or unreasonable actions, it will not be a measure in good faith.[25]

2 Non-Discriminatory

Under international law, States are not obliged to treat foreigners in the same way as their own nationals, as long as States do not breach the threshold of the international minimum standard. Foreigners are allowed to enter and stay subject to conditions decided by the State.[26] In the absence of specific treaty obligations, and as long as the State's actions do not slip under the international minimum standard, there is no obligation of non-discrimination on

---

23 *S.D. Myers, Inc. v Government of Canada*, Partial Award (13 November 2000), para 285; *Pope & Talbot Inc v. The Government of Canada*, Interim Award, UNCITRAL (26 June 2000), para 161.

24 *S.D. Myers, Inc. v Government of Canada*, Partial Award (13 November 2000), para 285; *Pope & Talbot Inc v. The Government of Canada*, Interim Award, UNCITRAL (26 June 2000), para 162, 195, 263.

25 Aniruddha Rajput, *Regulatory Freedom and Indirect Expropriation in Investment Arbitration* (Kluwer International, 2018), pp. 173–174.

26 Robert Jennings and Arthur Watts, ed., *Oppenheim's International Law*, vol. 1, 9th ed. (Harlow: Longman Group, 1992), pp. 897–900.

States.[27] The position was explained by the tribunal in *Methanex v USA* in the following words:

> As to the question of whether a rule of customary international law prohibits a State, in the absence of a treaty obligation, from differentiating in its treatment of nationals and aliens, international law is clear. In the absence of a contrary rule of international law binding on the States parties, whether of conventional or customary origin, a State may differentiate in its treatment of nationals and aliens.[28]

The FCN treaties tried to fill this gap by imposing the obligation of non-discrimination.[29] IIAs prohibit non-discrimination through fair and equitable treatment, most favoured national treatment (MFN) and national treatment (NT). The extent of non-discrimination imposed by IIAs is not absolute and qualified. It sufficient to include discrimination covered by MFN and NT. The scope of non-discrimination as an element of regulatory freedom is informed and developed with the case law on the treatment standards in IIAs that protect foreign investors from non-discrimination.

Non-discrimination is based on the idea of equality, nevertheless, it does not seek absolute equality.[30] Sometimes discrimination may be required to achieve equality.[31] The essence of the obligation of non-discrimination is that persons placed in similar situations shall not be discriminated against unless there are supervening grounds of public interest.[32] Therefore, it is possible that States can discriminate provided there are sufficient convincing policy

27 Ian Brownlie, *Principles of Public International Law* (7th ed., Oxford: Oxford University Press, 2008), pp. 524–528, 536–543.

28 *Methanex Corporation v. United States of America*, UNCITRAL, Award (3 August 2005), Part III, Chapter A, para. 25.

29 Rudolf Dolzer and Margarete Stevens, *Bilateral Investment Treaties* (Hague: Martinus Nijhoff Publishers, 1995) pp. 9–10.

30 *El Paso Energy International Company v. The Argentine Republic*, ICSID Case No. ARB/03/15, Award (31 October 2011), para. 305 citing A. F. M. Maniruzzaman, "Expropriation of Alien Property and the Principle of Non- Discrimination in International Law of Foreign Investment: An Overview," *J. Transnat'l L. & Pol'y* 8 (1998): 57.

31 M Sornarajah, *The Pursuit of Nationalized Property* (Dordrecht; Boston: Martinus Nijhoff, 1986), pp. 185–7; AFM Manuruzzaman, "Expropriation of Alien Property and the Principle of Non-Discrimination in International Law of Foreign Investment: An Overview" *Journal of Transnational Law and Policy* 8 (1998–9): 57, 58–62.

32 *Parkerings-Compegnite AS v Republic of Lithuania*, ICSID Case No. ARB/05/8, Award (11 September 2007), 411, 431, 441; UNCTAD, *Most-Favoured-Nation Treatment: UNCTAD Series on Issues in International Investment Agreements* (New York and Geneva: United Nations, 2010), pp. 27–28.

reasons, based on public interest. The presence of discrimination is decided based on whether entities alleged to be discriminated against are similarly placed with those in relation to whom they are alleged to be discriminated.

A regulation enacted in public interest can be discriminatory and yet may be a valid justification against non-discriminatory provisions since public policy considerations act as an exception. Thereby substantially narrowing the scope of the non-discrimination clause and leaving wide range of activities to be undertaken as a part of regulatory freedom.[33] If the discrimination is not based on nationality but is undertaken to achieve some public purpose, then it does not constitute breach of non-discrimination clauses. Treaty practice supports discrimination based on reasonable grounds in public interest. Such a measure does not constitute violation of MFN and NT.[34]

The presence of discrimination and its assessment is to be done based on "the circumstances of the individual cases".[35] Discrimination may be *de facto* or *de jure*. If the discrimination is factually established, it is *de facto* and if based on legislation it will be *de jure*.[36] In either case it is not necessary to establish the intention to discriminate as long as the 'effect' of discrimination is established it is sufficient.[37] Irrespective of the intention, discrimination exists if "objectively, two similar situations are not treated similarly."[38] Therefore, the test

33 *S.D. Myers, Inc. v Government of Canada*, para 250; *Emilio Agustín Maffezini v. The Kingdom of Spain*, ICSID Case No. ARB/97/7, Jurisdiction, (25 January 2000), para 62; *Parkerings-Compagniet AS v. Republic of Lithuania*, ICSID Case No. ARB/05/8, Award (11 September 2007), para. 368; Rudolf Dolzer and Margarete Stevens, *Bilateral Investment Treaties* (Hague: Martinus Nijhoff Publishers, 1995) p. 181.

34 Article 3, German Model BIT; Article 4 and Annexure B, Norway Model BIT. India-South Korea BIT (Signed on 26th February 1996, terminated on 12 May 2017) Art. 3; India-Tajikistan BIT (Signed on 13 December 1995, terminated on 22 March 2017) Art. 4; India-Italy BIT (Signed on 23 November 1995, terminated on 2017) Art. 3 (3); India-Malaysia BIT (Signed on 3 August 1995, terminated on 23 March 2017) Art. 5(1); Fredrico Ortino "Non-discriminatory Treatment in Investment Disputes" in *Human Rights in International Investment Law and Arbitration*, ed. Pierre-Marie Dupuy, Ernst-Ulrich Petersmann and Francesci Franiconi (Oxford: Oxford University Press, 2010),p. 361.

35 *Parkerings-Compagniet AS v. Republic of Lithuania*, ICSID Case No. ARB/05/8, Award (11 September 2007), para. 36.

36 *Total S.A. v. The Argentine Republic*, ICSID Case No. ARB/04/01, Decision on Liability (27 December 2010), paras. 212–3; Parkerings v Lithuania, para. 368.

37 *El Paso Energy International Company v. The Argentine Republic*, ICSID Case No. ARB/03/15, Award (31 October 2011), para. 305.

38 *Antoine Goetz et consorts v. République du Burundi*, ICSID Case No. ARB/95/3, Award (10 February 1999), para. 262; *El Paso Energy International Company v. The Argentine Republic*, ICSID Case No. ARB/03/15, Award (31 October 2011), para. 305.

of 'likeness' has become the critical factor in establishing discrimination.[39] While determining 'like circumstances' it is necessary to identify the competitor; the competitor and the investor are in the same economic or business sector and the difference must be an outcome of the measure of the State. The principle of non-discrimination requires "a State to treat equally what is equal but it does not require a State to treat equally that which is different."[40] Therefore "it is legally acceptable to provide for positive discrimination or reverse discrimination, which departs of the principle of formal equality in order to redress the situation of persons or groups when they deserve special protection through a reasonable preferential treatment."[41] The practical test identified in *AES v Hungary* is that discrimination "[d]iscrimination necessarily implies that the state benefited or harmed someone more in comparison with the generality."[42]

There may be several economic reasons forming the basis of public policy, which will justify different treatment across and within sectors.[43] The nature of the public interest involved may be such that the measures to be adopted may differ from one sector to another.[44] A rational basis for discrimination would be "a differential treatment based on the existence of a different factual and legal situation" and this "does not breach the BIT's standard."[45] It is natural to treat two entities in different sectors differently. It would be inappropriate to

39 *Goetz and others v. Burundi*, ICSID Case No. ARB/95/3, Award (February 10, 1999), para. 121; *Parkerings-Compagniet AS v. Republic of Lithuania*, ICSID Case No. ARB/05/8, Award (11 September 2007), para. 369.

40 *RREEF Infrastructure (G.P.) Limited and RREEF Pan-European Infrastructure Two Lux S.à r.l. v. Kingdom of Spain*, ICSID Case No. ARB/13/30, Decision on Responsibility and on the Principles of Quantum (30 November 2018), para. 431; *Nykomb Synergetics Technology Holding AB, Stockholm v The Republic of Latvia*, Award, The Arbitration Institute of Stockholm Chamber of Commerce (16 December 2003), para. 4.3.1; *BG Group Plc. v. Republic of Argentina*, UNCITRAL, Award (24 December 2007), para. 34.

41 *RREEF Infrastructure (G.P.) Limited and RREEF Pan-European Infrastructure Two Lux S.à r.l. v. Kingdom of Spain*, ICSID Case No. ARB/13/30, Decision on Responsibility and on the Principles of Quantum (30 November 2018), para. 431.

42 *AES Summit Generation Limited and AES-Tisza Erömü Kft v. The Republic of Hungary*, ICSID Case No. ARB/07/22, Award, (23 September 2010), para. 10.3.53.

43 *Total S.A. v. The Argentine Republic*, ICSID Case No. ARB/04/01, Decision on Liability (27 December 2010), paras. 212–4.

44 *El Paso Energy International Company v. The Argentine Republic*, ICSID Case No. ARB/03/15, Award (31 October 2011), para. 311.

45 *El Paso Energy International Company v. The Argentine Republic*, ICSID Case No. ARB/03/15, Award, (31 October 2011), para. 315.

suggest that mere differential treatment across different sectors means meting out a harsh treatment by singling out a certain sector.[46]

There is no breach of investment treaty if two sectors are treated differently in a regulation, as long as there is no "capricious, irrational or absurd differentiation in the treatment accorded to the Claimant as compared to other entities or sectors."[47] The non-discrimination obligation does not operate across the entire economy allowing comparison between investors in two different sectors. As explained in *El Paso v Argentina*,

> *foreign investors* are protected against discrimination does not entail the far-reaching consequence that a State cannot treat differently the economic actors in different sectors of the economy, as long as this differential treatment applies equally to national and foreign investors.[48]

If the treatment received was the same as it was received by other participants of the same sector, whether foreign or national, then there is no discrimination.[49] Entities in different sectors may be subject to different regulations. Because "[t]reating different categories of subjects differently is not unequal treatment. The principle of equality only applies between equal subjects, not between unequal subjects."[50] It is an integral part of the power of the State to create its legal system and competent authorities whereby it can "establish different rules to govern different subjects."[51]

Discrimination may take various forms such as race, religion, political affiliation, disability and various other criteria.[52] In the context of investment arbitration, it takes place primarily on the basis of nationality, although other

---

46 *Sempra Energy International v. Argentine Republic*, ICSID Case No. ARB/02/16, Award (September 28 2007), para. 319.

47 *Enron Creditors Recovery Corporation (formerly Enron Corporation) and Ponderosa Assets, L.P. v. Argentine Republic*, ICSID Case No. ARB/01/3, para. 282; *El Paso Energy International Company v. The Argentine Republic*, ICSID Case No. ARB/03/15, Award (31 October 2011), para. 315.

48 *El Paso Energy International Company v. The Argentine Republic*, ICSID Case No. ARB/03/15, Award (31 October 2011), para. 306.

49 *El Paso Energy International Company v. The Argentine Republic*, ICSID Case No. ARB/03/15, Award (31 October 2011), paras. 306, 308.

50 *Metalpar S.A. and Buen Aire S.A. v. The Argentine Republic*, ICSID Case No. ARB/03/5, Award on the Merits (Unofficial English Translation) (6 June 2008), para. 162.

51 *Metalpar S.A. and Buen Aire S.A. v. The Argentine Republic*, ICSID Case No. ARB/03/5, Award on the Merits (Unofficial English Translation) (6 June 2008), para. 162.

52 Warwick McKean, *Equality and Discrimination under Intentional Law* (Oxford: Clarendon Press, 1983), p. 11.

forms also exist. Certain discriminations such as racial discrimination are *ex faci* bad since they cannot be defended on public policy grounds.[53]

In any event, the overall scheme of the regulations is to be seen since there may be "the objective of balancing for each sector the advantages and disadvantages of the general economic situation."[54] Two investors may not be in like circumstances, despite similarities in objective and venue because of their respective sizes and location, which would have a different effect on their profitability.[55] However, if there are grounds to justify different treatment of investors, then that would not be 'like circumstances'.[56] Additionally, a cumulative reading of the UN practice shows that discriminatory treatment is allowed in the following cases: a) protective measures to promote welfare of particular indigenous groups; b) the measures must be wanted by these groups; c) based on the needs of particular groups and not race or colour or classification; and d) not be continued for longer than strictly necessary.[57]

It is clear from the jurisprudence of investment tribunals that every discrimination does not result in breach if the IIA.[58] For a discrimination to "violate international law, discrimination must be unreasonable or lacking proportionality, for instance, it must be inapposite or excessive to achieve an otherwise legitimate objective of the State. An objective justification may justify differentiated treatments of similar cases. It would be necessary, in each case, to evaluate the exact circumstances and the context."[59] Explaining the possibility of regulatory freedom acting as an exception the tribunal in *Parkerings v Lithuania* stated that:

> No policy or purpose behind the said measure must apply to the investment that justifies the different treatments accorded. *A contrario*, a less favourable treatment is acceptable if a State's legitimate objective

53 M Sornarajah, *International Law on Foreign Investment*, 3rd ed. (Cambridge: Cambridge University Press, 2010), pp. 409–10.

54 *El Paso Energy International Company v. The Argentine Republic*, ICSID Case No. ARB/03/15, Award (31 October 2011), para. 310.

55 *Parkerings-Compagniet AS v. Republic of Lithuania*, ICSID Case No. ARB/05/8, Award (11 September 2007), para. 396.

56 *Parkerings-Compagniet AS v. Republic of Lithuania*, ICSID Case No. ARB/05/8, Award (11 September 2007), para. 374.

57 Warwick McKean, *Equality and Discrimination under Intentional Law* (Oxford: Clarendon Press, 1983), p. 91.

58 *El Paso Energy International Company v. The Argentine Republic*, ICSID Case No. ARB/03/15, Award (31 October 2011), para. 305.

59 *Parkerings-Compegnite AS v Republic of Lithuania*, ICSID Case No. ARB/05/8, Award (11 September 2007), para. 368.

justifies such different treatment in relation to the specificity of the investment.[60]

3 Public Interest

A regulatory measure must be undertaken to achieve a clear and tangible public interest or public purpose. The very reason for the existence of a State is to protect and uphold public interest; public interest is dubbed as the highest goal – the phrase *salas populi supreme lex* captures this ethos.[61] The range of public interests for which regulations ought to be exercised is diverse and extensive. It is impossible to exhaustively define or enumerate a comprehensive list of public interests that need protection – neither in a treaty or otherwise. Also, the public interest and the priorities amongst different public interests would change over time. If the only basis of concern for governmental action was public interest there is nothing wrong with such a regulation. The choice of the public policy and the extent of its concern will be different for one State than another. As succulently put by Judge Spender: "it cannot be determined within a formula. It is a conception."[62] It would be the duty of the claimant to establish otherwise.[63]

States have the discretion to decide the measure they need to undertake to uphold public interest, unless the action of the government is clearly arbitrary.[64] The state has to establish that the necessary conditions for the exercise of the discretion to choose the public interest it wishes to preserve exist.[65] The public purpose that a society wises to preserve would depend on the priorities of the society concerned and shall be decided with "reference

60 *Parkerings-Compegnite AS v Republic of Lithuania*, ICSID Case No. ARB/05/8, Award (11 September 2007), para. 371.

61 *Great Venezuelan Railroad Case* (1903) 10 RIAA 468, 472–3; Bin Cheng, *General Principles of Law as Applied by International Courts and Tribunals* (London: Stevens and Sons, 1953), pp. 30–31.

62 *Application of the Convention of 1902 Governing the Guardianship of Infants (Netherlands v. Sweden)*, Judgment (Separate Opinion of Sir Percy Spender) [1958] ICJ Reports 55 (28 November 1958) 122.

63 *David Minnotte and Robert Lewis v. Republic of Poland*, ICSID Case No. ARB(AF)/10/1, Award (*16 May 2014), para. 171.

64 *Lozar Rokash Case*, American Turkish Claims Settlement (1937) *Nielson's Opinion and Reports* 503, 509; *Hochbaum Case, Upper Silesian Arbitral Tribunal* (1934) 5 Collection of Decisions 140, 162; Werner Levi, *The International Ordre Public* (1994) 57 Revue de Droit International 57, 66–7; *Kuwait Air Corporation* 116 ILR 571, 323.

65 *Faber Case* (1903) Ven Arb 600, 626, 630.

to the society's current standard of reasonably acceptable behavior."[66] The PCIJ explained the deference towards determinations of municipal courts on the ground that these are "sensitive matters" of "public policy" on which only the municipal courts are competent and equipped to comment.[67] Noting the "wide regulatory space", the tribunal in *Thunderbird v Mexico* stated that on issues of public policy – "reflecting national views on public morals". The host States are free to change their regulatory framework for achievement of these public policy objectives.[68] It is only exceptional that an investment tribunal will decide contrary to the considered view of the local authorities.[69]

Public interest is often covered under the broad rubric of "public security and order, public health and morality."[70] Some of the prominent areas of public interest are climate change, environment protection, human rights, labour standards, health safety, protection of public morals, prevention of corruption etc.[71] Issues of public interest may arise from an international obligation arising out of a treaty or customary obligation[72] or domestic law priorities such as protection of intellectual property rights and prevention of smuggling[73] or ensuring a certain sector stays only in the hands of solvent enterprises.[74]

In *Quasar de Valors v Russia*, the tribunal expressed the need to prioritize the interest of investors over public interest in the following words:

---

66 Thomas Waelde & Abba Kolo, "Environmental Regulation, Investment Protection and 'Regulatory Taking' in International Law" *International & Comparative Law Quarterly* 50 (2001): 811, 827.

67 *Payment of Various Serbian Loans Issued by France* (*France v Kingdom of Serbs, Crovates and Slovanes*), 1929 PCIJ (Series A) No. 20 (12 July 1929). p. 46.

68 *International Thunderbird Gaming Corporation v. The United Mexican States*, UNCITRAL, 2005, para 50, 127, 202, *Emilio Augustín Maffezini v. The Kingdom of Spain*, ICSID Case No. ARB/97/7, Decision on the Tribunal on Objections to Jurisdiction, (25 January 2000).

69 *Blusun S.A., Jean-Pierre Lecorcier and Michael Stein v. Italian Republic*, ICSID Case No. ARB/14/3, Final Award (27 December 2016), para. 318.

70 *Philip Morris Products S.A. and Abal Hermanos S.A. v. Oriental Republic of Uruguay*, ICSID Case No. ARB/10/7, Award (8 July 2016), para. 291.

71 For a summary of the public interest issues raised in arbitrations see Yulia Levashova, *The Right of States to Regulate in International Investment Law: The Search for Balance Between Public Interest and Fair and Equitable Treatment*, (Kluwer Law International, 2019), pp. 199–202; Aniruddha Rajput, *Regulatory Freedom and Indirect Expropriation in Investment Arbitration* (Kluwer International, 2018), pp. 178–183.

72 *S.D. Myers, Inc. v Government of Canada*, UNCITRAL, para 255.

73 *Marvin Feldman v Mexico*, Award, ICSID Case No. ARB (AF)/99/1 (16 December 2002), para 170.

74 *Gami Investments, Inc. v. The Government of the United Mexican States*, UNCITRAL, Final Award (15 November 2004), para 114.

> Moreover, where the value of an investment has been substantially impaired by state action, albeit a bona fide regulation in the public interest, one can see the force in the proposition that investment protection treaties might not allow a host state to place such a high individual burden on a foreign investor to contribute, without the payment of compensation, to the accomplishment of regulatory objectives for the benefit of a national community of which the investor is not a member.[75]

Once an investor makes a sunk-in investment, the investor is very much a part of the local community. The presence of additional protection through IIAs does not make an investor immune to public interest in the community where it operates. Even major corporations and businesses would not take such a position. In the case of regulatory freedom, the public interest is the interest of the entire community. If the measure is not geared towards achieving public interest or the public interest is not genuine in the first place, good faith will be absent and the measure will not satisfy the requirements of regulatory freedom.

4 Due Process

Whether treated as a part of regulatory freedom or not, due process may be pertinent as an element of fair and equitable treatment. Broadly speaking, due process is linked to other elements of regulatory freedom discussed above. In relation to regulatory freedom, due process will require the State to adhere to procedural propriety.[76] The fair and equitable treatment, for example, requires compliance with "well-established fundamental standards as good faith, due process, and non-discrimination."[77] A regulatory measure will have to satisfy this standard of due process. There are various approaches towards due process as a part of FET, ranging from due process as specified in the *Neer case* to much

75 *Quasar de Valors SICAV S.A. and others (formerly Renta 4 S.V.S.A and others) v. Russia*, SCC Case No. 24/2007, Award (20 July 2012), para. 23.

76 *International Thunderbird Gaming Corporation v. The United Mexican States*, UNCITRAL Award (26 January 2006), paras. 197–201. Also see Ursula Kriebaum, Christoph Schreuer, Rudolf Dolzer, *Principles of International Investment Law* (3rd edn: Oxford University Press, 2022), pp. 219–22.

77 *Saluka Investments B.V. v. The Czech Republic*, UNCITRAL, Partial Award, 17 March 2006, para. 303 (footnote excluded).

broader approaches.[78] Despite these various approaches "a high threshold of severity and gravity is required" to establish absence of due process under the fair and equitable treatment standard; whether this assessment takes place in relation to the international minimum standard or otherwise.[79]

International courts and tribunals, other than investment tribunals have not included due process into the elements of regulatory freedom. In investment arbitration cases there is a direct interaction between the investor and the host State and the investor is affected by the decision of the host State. The decision-making process therefore becomes an integral part of the determination of regulatory freedom. Largely, due process is an aspect of good faith – testing whether the action was arbitrary or unreasonable. There can be exacting standards that can be applied. As long as the State follows a fair procedure that constitutes a sufficient evidence of due process.[80] There are divergent views about the need to consult and the extent of consultation with foreign investors. Tribunals range from treating a communication to the business bodies to be sufficient to specific consultation with the investor.[81] The tribunal in *Thunderbird v Mexico* stated that since the investor was allowed to make representations due process was present.[82] There are instances where the tribunals have held that there is no need to consult as in light of the circumstances and the nature of the measure.[83] The determination will have to be made based on the circumstances including the urgency of the measure, resources of the State, extent and limits on engagement with the industry and specific investors.

78 For a summary of different approaches in the case law see *Apotex Holdings Inc. and Apotex Inc. v. United States of America*, ICSID Case No. ARB(AF)/12/1, Award (25 August 2014), paras. 9.42–9.46.

79 *Apotex Holdings Inc. and Apotex Inc. v. United States of America*, ICSID Case No. ARB(AF)/12/1, Award (25 August 2014), para. 9.47.

80 Ursula Kriebaum, Christoph Schreuer, Rudolf Dolzer, *Principles of International Investment Law* (3rd edn: Oxford University Press, 2022), p. 221.

81 Caroline Henckels, "A Duty to Consult Foreign Investors When Changing the Regulatory Framework? Implications for Non-Communicable Disease Prevention and Beyond" JWIT 21 (2020): 698, 704–710.

82 *International Thunderbird Gaming Corporation v. The United Mexican States*, UNCITRAL Award (26 January 2006), paras 197–201.

83 *Sergei Paushok, CJSC Golden East Company and CJSC Vostokneftegaz Company v Mongolia*, UNCITRAL, Award on Jurisdiction and Liability (28 April 2011), para 304; *Renée Rose Levy de Levi v Republic of Peru*, ICSID Case No ARB/10/17, Award (26 February 2014), paras 183, 389.

A State is entitled to undertake a measure and not breach its obligations under an IIA if its measures satisfy the requirements of *bona fide*, non-discriminatory, public interest and due process. These requirements emerge from customary international law and the principles of conflict of norms allows it to stand unaffected, despite the presence of treatment standards.

CHAPTER 7

Standard of Review

The preceding chapter set out the elements of regulatory freedom. While it comes to the application of regulatory freedom, the question of the standard of review to be applied becomes equally relevant. If the standard of review is too strict and extracting, a measure will not be categories as regulatory freedom. If it is too flexible, several regulations will easily pass the test making the standard of protection nebulous. The standard of review applied in the current practice of investment tribunals and the appropriate standard to apply are discussed in the following sections.

Regulatory freedom is not self-judging therefore, the authority of investment tribunals to review the measures of the State, to test whether that measure accords with the criteria set out in customary international law is not excluded. Unless, an IIA expressly excludes the review by the tribunal or identifies another authority with that competence, the discretion of the tribunals is unaffected. It is true that investment tribunals do not have in-depth knowledge of local conditions and should not second guess governmental decisions. But that "does not prevent a tribunal from evaluating how the measure that lawmakers selected comports with the state's international obligations."[1] Standard of review is the extent of scrutiny an international tribunal will apply to investigate whether the State's measure falls within the permissible limits of the international obligation in question.[2] In other words, the standard of review is the sphere of discretion or the degree of deference in favour of a State, while acting within which a State will not breach its international obligations.[3] Since regulatory freedom will be claimed by a State, the burden will be firstly on the State, and once established *prima facie*, it would shift on the claimant to

1 *Olympic Entertainment Group AS v. Republic of Ukraine*, PCA Case No. 2019-18, Award (15 April 2021), para. 95.

2 Jan Bohanes and Nicholas Lockhart, "Standard of Review in WTO Law" in *The Oxford Handbook of International Trade Law*, ed. Daniel Bethleham and others, (Oxford: Oxford University Press, 2009), p. 378–9; Lukasz Gruszczynski, Wouter Werner, "Introduction" in *Deference in International Courts and Tribunals: Standard of Review and Margin of Appreciation*, ed. Lukasz Gruszczynski and Wouter Werner (Oxford: Oxford University Press, 2014), pp. 3–4.

3 Chiara Ragni, "Standard of Review and the Margin of Appreciation before the International Court of Justice" in *Deference in International Courts and Tribunals: Standard of Review and Margin of Appreciation*, ed. Lukasz Gruszczynski and Wouter Werner, (Oxford: Oxford University Press, 2014), p. 320.

 | DOI:10.1163/9789004759831_008

prove that the Respondent's actions were inconsistent with legitimate exercise of regulatory freedom.[4]

A variety of standards exist in international law and different standards have been applied by investment tribunals.[5] The prominent ones applied by investment tribunals are necessity and proportionality without much elaboration on the concept, elements and the scope of review conducted under these standards.[6] This sub-section investigates the appropriateness of these standards and especially good faith review which is applied when a treaty is silent on the standard of review to be applied. Needless to add stricter the standard lesser is the scope of regulatory freedom since a regulatory measure would be readily treated to be in breach of treaty obligations; and vice versa.

1 Necessity and Proportionality

Proportionality is the most frequently referred standard for review of regulatory freedom in investment arbitration.[7] Strictly speaking, proportionality is a part of necessity. Necessity is a broader concept that encompasses

4 *Les Laboratoires Servier, S.A.S., Biofarma, S.A.S. and Arts et Techniques du Progres S.A.S. v. Republic of Poland*, UNCITRAL, Award (14 February 2012), paras. 582–4.

5 Caroline Henckels, "The Role of the Standard of Review and the Importance of Deference in Investor-State Arbitration" in *Deference in International Courts and Tribunals: Standard of Review and Margin of Appreciation*, ed. Lukasz Gruszczynski and Wouter Wermer, (Oxford: Oxford University Press, 2014), pp. 117–120.

6 *Técnicas Medioambientales Tecmed, S.A. v. The United Mexican States*, ICSID Case No. ARB (AF)/00/2, Award (29 May 2003), paras 117–19, 121–22; *LG&E Energy Corp., LG&E Capital Corp., LG&E International Inc v Argentine Republic*, ICSID Case No. ARB/02/1, Decision on Liability (3 October 2006), paras 177, 189–95; *Azurix Corporation v The Argentine Republic*, ICSID Case No. ARB/01/12, Award (14 July 2006), at paras 310–12; *Suez, Sociedad General de Aguas de Barcelona S.A., and InterAgua Servicios Integrales del Agua S.A. v Argentne Republic*, ICSID Case No. ARB/03/17, Decision on Liability (30 July 2010), paras 215–7; *Glamis Gold Ltd. v United States of America*, UNCITRAL (NAFTA), Award (8 June 2009), at paras 624–25, 726, 761–71, 779, 803–05; *Deutsche Bank AG v. Democratic Socialist Republic of Sri Lanka*, ICSID Case No. ARB/09/2, Award (31 October 2012), para 522; *Occidental Petroleum Corporation and Occidental Exploration and Production Company v. Republic of Ecuador*, ICSID Case No. ARB/06/11, Award (5 October 2012), paras 402–3.

7 *Total S.A. v. The Argentine Republic*, ICSID Case No. ARB/04/01, Decision on Liability (27 December 2010), para. 123; *RREEF Infrastructure (G.P.) Limited and RREEF Pan-European Infrastructure Two Lux S.à r.l. v. Kingdom of Spain*, ICSID Case No. ARB/13/30, Decision on Responsibility and on the Principles of Quantum (30 November 2018), para. 468; *El Paso Energy International Company v. Argentine Republic*, ICSID Case No. ARB/03/15, Award (31 October 2011), para. 241; *Olympic Entertainment Group AS v. Republic of Ukraine*, PCA Case No. 2019-18, Award (15 April 2021), para. 90.

proportionality. There has been some inconsistency in the application of necessity by courts and tribunals but broadly, three elements have been identified most often: suitability, necessity and proportionality *sensu stricto*.[8]

Suitability is the first element of necessity and it involves an assessment of two situations: whether the purpose of the objective of the measure is legitimate and the measure undertaken is suitable to protect the interest which the measure purports to protect.[9] Normally, if a measure is adopted in good faith, the measure by itself is suitable and the two situations are satisfied.[10] This is the standard of review that the ICJ applies where treaties do not specify any particular standard of review.

The second stage is necessity whereby it is investigated whether alternative ways were available to achieve the same outcome in the least restrictive manner.[11] Although the same term 'necessity' is used. The general reference to necessity implies the standard of review and as an element of the general reference, necessity implies investigation of whether alternative methods were available to achieve the same goal. This stage involves a rigorous review as compared to the first stage of suitability, which is a good faith review. Necessity as the second state of review is applied as an independent standard of review during the interpretation of General Exceptions in Article XX of the GATT and state of necessity under Article 25 of the Articles on State Responsibility. In both situations there is textual support for their application and they refer to necessity as an exceptional remedy. This characteristic has made its

8 *United States – Measures Affecting the Cross-Border Supply of Gambling and Betting Services*, Appellate Body Report, WT/DS285/AB/R (7 April 2005), paras. 294, 306–307; Jan Jans, 'Proportionality Revisited' Legal Issues of Economic Integration 27, no. 3 (2000): 239, 240–241.

9 Jan Jans, 'Proportionality Revisited' Legal Issues of Economic Integration 27, no. 3 (2000): 239, 240–241.

10 Andreas Kulick, *Global Public Interest in International Investment Law* (Cambridge: Cambridge University Press, 2012), pp. 186–187.

11 *Canada – Measures Relating to Exports of Wheat and Treatment of Imported Grain*, WT/DS276, Reports of the Panel (6 April 2004), para. 6.226; *European Communities – Protection of Trademarks and Geographical Indications for Agricultural Products and Foodstuffs* (US), Panel Reports, WT/DS290, paras. 7.458–7.460; *Dominican Republic – Measures Affecting the Importation and Internal Sale of Cigarettes*, WT/DS302, para. 70; *Thailand – Restrictions on Importation of and Internal Taxes on Cigarettes*, GATT Panel Report, GATT BISD (DS10/R – 37S/200) (7 November 1990), 223; *United States – Section 337 of the Tariff Act of 1930*, GATT Panel Report, GATT BISD (L/6439–36S/345 36th Sup.) (7 November 1989), 345; *United States – Standards for Reformulated and Conventional Gasoline*, Panel Report, WT/DS2, paras. 6.26 and 6.28; *Brazil – Measures Affecting Imports of Retreaded Tyres*, WT/DS332, para. 172; *Canada-Terms of Patent Protection*, Report of the Appellate Body, WT/DS170/AB/R (18 September 2000), para. 6.226.

successful invocation almost impossible. The ICJ has applied necessity only where the text or the substantive rule of international law supports its application. Without a specific reference in the primary rule, whether contained in a treaty or customary international law, the ICJ has refrained from invoking it. The prominent examples of application of necessity are, of course, Article 25 of the Articles on State Responsibility,[12] necessity and proportionality as a requirement for valid exercise of the right of self-defense,[13] and under international humanitarian law where the attack has to be proportional to the advantage while attacking a military target.[14] The ICJ has not applied the necessity test outside of these situations.

The problem with the application of necessity in the absence of support in the text of the treaty or underlying substantive provision is that it is a *post facto* analysis of State measures. The alternatives proposed would depend on the ingenuity of pleadings and none of those alternatives were before the decision-making authorities. The unviability of the second test was noted by the tribunal in *El Paso v Argentina*. The nature of certain situations is such that States are doing no more than responding to a situation. The government would have to decide the most viable option in the circumstances, within the political and economic considerations and pressures of a given situation.[15] The tribunal in *Philip Morris v Uruguay* was explicit in this regard:

> For a country with limited technical and economic resources, such as Uruguay, adhesion to the FCTC and involvement in the process of scientific and technical cooperation and reporting and of exchange of information represented an important if not indispensable means for acquiring the scientific knowledge and market experience needed for the proper implementation of its obligations under the FCTC and for ensuring the fulfilment of its tobacco control policy.[16]

The third stage is proportionality *stricto sensu*. It involves an evaluation and balance of the losses suffered by the claimant and the public interest that was

---

12 *Gabčíkovo-Nagymaros Project (Hungary/Slovakia)*, Judgment, [1997] ICJ Reports 7, (25 September 1997) para 85.

13 *Military and Paramilitary Activities in and against Nicaragua (Nicaragua v United States of America)*, [1986] ICJ Reports 14 (27 June 1986), paras. 194, 237, 249.

14 *Armed Activities on the Territory of the Congo (Democratic Republic of the Congo v Uganda)*, Judgment, [2005] ICJ Reports 168 (19 December 2005), para 147.

15 *El Paso Energy International Company v. The Argentine Republic*, ICSID Case No. ARB/03/15, Award (31 October 2011), para. 320.

16 *Philip Morris Products S.A. and Abal Hermanos S.A. v. Oriental Republic of Uruguay*, ICSID Case No. ARB/10/7, Award (8 July 2016), para. 393.

ultimately achieved or sought to be achieved.[17] Here proportionality operates in a manner that the benefits accrued to the society shall be proportional to the costs to be borne by the individual.

Proportionality as applied in investment arbitration has originated in European Court of Human Rights (ECtHR) and was initially applied while assessing the expropriation standard.[18] Proportionality was introduced in investment arbitration in *Techmed v Mexico*. The tribunal relied on the jurisprudence of the ECtHR to introduce proportionality into investment arbitration case-law.[19] The tribunal stated that:

> After establishing that regulatory actions and measures will not be initially excluded from the definition of expropriatory acts, in addition to the negative financial impact of such actions or measures, the Arbitral Tribunal will consider, in order to determine if they are to be characterized as expropriatory, whether such actions or measures are proportional to the public interest presumably protected thereby and to the protection legally granted to investments, taking into account that the significance of such impact has a key role upon deciding the proportionality ... There must be a *reasonable relationship of proportionality between the charge or weight imposed to the foreign investor and the aim sought to be realized* by any expropriatory measure.[20] [emphasis added]

This is proportionality *stricto sensu*, the one in the strictest form.[21]

Proportionality has been applied by the ECtHR based on the right to property that was introduced as a human right into the European human rights system through Protocol 1 to the European Convention on Human Rights (ECHR).[22] In the famous *Sporrong and Lönnroth* case ECtHR held that due to the nature of right to property (as a human right) under the ECHR there is

---

17 *Korea – Measures Affecting Imports of Fresh, Chilled and Frozen Beef*, WT/DS161, Appellate Body Report (11 December 2000), WT/DS161/AB/R, para. 164.

18 August Reinisch, "Expropriation" in *The Oxford Handbook of International Investment Law*, ed. Peter T Muchlinski, Federico Ortino, Christoph Schreuer (Oxford University Press, 2008), pp. 449–50.

19 *El Paso Energy International Company v. The Argentine Republic*, ICSID Case No. ARB/03/15, Award, 31 October 2011, para. 243.

20 *Técnicas Medioambientales Tecmed, S.A. v. The United Mexican States*, ICSID Case No. ARB (AF)/00/2, Award (29 May 2003), para. 122.

21 The tribunal in *El Paso v Argentina* also applied proportionality as applied under the ECHR by relying on *Techmed v Mexico*. *El Paso Energy International Company v. The Argentine Republic*, ICSID Case No. ARB/03/15, Award (31 October 2011), para. 243.

22 Christoph Grabenwarter, *European Convention on Human Rights: Commentary* (Germany: C.H. Beck, Hart, Nomos, Helbing Lichtenhahn Verlag, 2014), pp. 367–388.

a need to strike a balance between individual and collective interests hence the community interest achieved has to be assessed in light of the impact on the individual.[23] Outside of the ECHR context, the so-called right to property does not have the same elevated status.[24] Hence there are doubts about the appropriateness of the application of proportionality *stricto sensu*.

Both necessity and proportionality have their inherent problems. Being an outcome of judicial decisions, their elements are not always clearly set out or applied. Even with the European framework, sometimes proportionality is applied as a basis to decline jurisdiction whereas on other occasions used as a justification for the violation of substantive provisions of the ECHR.[25] They are unsuitable for investment arbitration.[26] In *Philip Morris v Uruguay*, the need to assess the proportionality of the benefits of the measure with the impact on the investor was not entertained.[27] The problem with such an assessment is that a general regulatory measure will inevitably impact individual investor. Moreover, the impact will be different on different investors because the target of the measures are not the investor but the public interest sought to be protected. States have the power to adopt their policies through regulations "having a social or general welfare purpose" therefore, a State would not incur liability for such regulations "except in cases where the State's action is obviously disproportionate to the need being addressed."[28] The effect of the measure on the investor is not a pertinent consideration.

2 Good Faith Review

What most investment tribunals call as proportionality is in fact a good faith review which is the standard normally applied by international courts and

23 *Sporrong and Lönnroth v Sweden*, ECHR, Judgment, Ser A No. 52, (23 September 1982), para. 73.

24 John Sprankling, *The International Law of Property* (Oxford: Oxford University Press, 2014), pp. 8–16, 104–206; Aniruddha Rajput, *Regulatory Freedom and Indirect Expropriation in Investment Arbitration* (Kluwer International, 2018), pp. 92–97.

25 Yuval Shany, "Towards a General Margin of Appreciation Doctrine in International Law?" *European Journal of International Law*16 (2005): 907, 909–914; George Letsas, "Two Concepts of the Margin of Appreciation" *Oxford Journal of Legal Studies* 26 (2006): 705, 706–715.

26 For further points see Aniruddha Rajput, *Regulatory Freedom and Indirect Expropriation in Investment Arbitration* (Kluwer International, 2018), pp. 188–190.

27 *Philip Morris Products S.A. and Abal Hermanos S.A. v. Oriental Republic of Uruguay*, ICSID Case No. ARB/10/7, Award (8 July 2016), para 144, 176.

28 *LG&E Energy Corp., LG&E Capital Corp. and LG&E International Inc. v. Argentine Republic*, Decision on Liability, ICSID Case No. ARB/02/1, para. 195.

tribunals if no other standard is specified. For example, as per the tribunal in *AES v Hungary* the thrust of proportionality is on "a reasonable correlation between the state's policy objective and the measures adopted to achieve it".[29] The investment tribunals do not define proportionality but simply declare that they are applying proportionality and the version of proportionality they apply often involves an assessment of the legitimacy of the objective and whether the measure is capable to achieve the objective. Actually this twin test constitutes a good faith review.

The ICJ has used this standard in two situations: *fist*, the underlying treaty is silent on the standard of review; *second*, a regulatory measure has been alleged to have violated treaty obligations.[30] According to the ICJ, if the underling treaty or the customary international law rule is silent, the standard to be applied is of good faith review.[31] The genesis of the good faith review is that all exercises of discretion, if not barred by the treaty shall be performed in good faith and in a reasonable manner.[32]

There is a link between good faith and reasonableness whereby good faith is a broader concept covering reasonableness. Good faith obligation will be violated if the actions are manifestly unreasonable.[33] At the same time, the exercise of discretion by a State shall be reasonable.[34] Reasonableness, as a part of good faith review requires that there is a reasonable relationship

---

29 *AES Summit Generation Limited and AES-Tisza Erömü Kft v. The Republic of Hungary*, ICSID Case No. ARB/07/22, Award (23 September 2010), para. 10.3.35.

30 *Elettronica Sicula S.p.A. (ELSI) (United States of America v. Italy)*, Judgment [1989] ICJ Reports 15, (20 July 1989), para 129, p 76; Bin Cheng, *General Principles of Law as Applied by International Courts and Tribunals* (London: Stevens and Sons, 1953), pp. 128–129.

31 *Certain Questions of Mutual Assistance in Criminal Matters (Djibouti v. France)*, Judgment, [2008] ICJ Reports 177 (4 June 2008), para 145; *Case Concerning the Barcelona Traction, Light and Power Company, Limited (New Application: 1962) (Belgium v. Spain) Second Phase*, [1970] ICJ Reports 3 (5 February 1970), para 9; *Gabíkovo-Nagymaros Project (Hungary v Slovakia)*, Judgment, [1997] ICJ Rep. 7 (25 September 1997), para 142; *Case Concerning Territorial Dispute (Libya Arab Jamahiriya/Chad)*, Judgment, [1994] ICJ Reports 6 (3 February 1994), para 51; *Jurisdictional Immunities of the State (Germany v Italy)*, Judgememt, [2012] ICJ Reports 99, para 137; For practice of ICJ see John f O'Connor, *Good Faith in International Law* (Aldershot, Dartmouth Publishing, 1991), p. 81.

32 *Rights of Nationals of the United States of America in Morocco (France v. United States of America)*, Judgment, (1952) ICJ Reports 176 (27 August 1952), 212; Nicaragua, Merits, paras. 419–20.

33 *Fisheries Case (United Kingdom v. Norway)*, Judgment (1951) ICJ Reports 116 (18 December 1951), 141–2.

34 Oliver Corten, "Reasonableness in International Law" in *Max Planck Encyclopedia of Public International Law*, ed. Rüdiger Wolfrum (New York: Oxford University Press, 2008), paras 2,7.

between the measures and its goal.[35] A measure would not be arbitrary if it is a reasonable response to achieve a certain public purpose.[36] It need not be in the relationship of necessity or proportionate that is there is no need to find if there were alternate options available or that the effect on the investor is larger than the effect on the public interest. Reasonableness and good faith ensure that the measure is not disguised. It is distinct from the substantive requirement of god faith because each of the ingredients of the regulatory freedom that is public interest and non-discrimination are then to be verified on the touch stone of good faith.

The ICJ applied the same test in the *Whaling* case. Both the parties to the dispute agreed that as per the standard of review of reasonableness, the decision shall be objectively reasonable or supported by coherent reasoning thus objectively justifiable.[37] The Court noted that it has to see that the "design and implementation are reasonable in relation to achieving its stated objectives. This standard of review is an objective one."[38] The decision of reasonableness will depend on facts and circumstances and all these factors have to be considered cumulatively.[39]

There are limits on the extent of assessment an international tribunal can do of the objective, and the measures taken to achieve the objective. It will be impractical and unreasonable to conduct an exacting inquiry. An international court or tribunal is neither sufficiently equipped nor fully informed about the local situations in with such a discretion has been exercised. The ICJ acknowledged this position in the *Navigation Rights* case in the following words:

> Further, a court examining the reasonableness of a regulation must recognize that the regulator, in this case the State with sovereignty over the river, has the primary responsibility for assessing the need for regulation and for choosing, on the basis of its knowledge of the situation, the measure that it deems most appropriate to meet that need. It will not be enough in a challenge to a regulation simply to assert in a general way

35 *Dispute Regarding Navigational and Related Rights* (*Costa Rica v Nicaragua*) (2009) ICJ Reports 213 (13 July 2009), para. 87 (a).

36 *Philip Morris Brand SARL, Philip Morris Products S.A. and Abal Hermanos S.A. v. Oriental Republic of Uruguay*, ICSID Case No. ARB/10/7, Award (8 July 2016), para. 391.

37 *Whaling in the Antarctic* (*Australia v. Japan: New Zealand intervening*), Judgment, [2014] ICJ Reports 226 (31 March 2014), para 66.

38 *Whaling in the Antarctic* (*Australia v. Japan: New Zealand intervening*), Judgment, [2014] ICJ Reports 226 (31 March 2014), para 67.

39 *The "Camouco" Case* (*Panama v France*), *Application for Prompt Release*, Judgment, ITLOS, List of Cases No. 5 (7 February 2000), paras 65–70.

> that it is unreasonable. Concrete and specific facts will be required to persuade a court to come to that conclusion.[40]

Investment tribunals have applied various tests to ensure that a reasonable and balance approach is taken. The measure, the rationale behind the measure and the effect of the measure is to be seen in the overall context of the sector and the area sought to be regulated. It is not always possible to establish a clear relationship between the measure and the goal.[41] The twin test of reasonableness of the goal and a reasonable relationship between the goal and the measure will be satisfied "as long as the changes are not capricious or unnecessary and do not amount to suddenly and unpredictably eliminate the essential characteristics of the existing regulatory framework."[42] And, "the modifications are not random, unnecessary or arbitrary, that is, provided that they do not significantly modify the legal framework applicable to the investors."[43] The tribunals appear to be applying a general test of reasonableness to find out there is a link between the measure and the goal, including an analysis of the intention of the legislature.[44]

Since a good faith review is not an exacting inquiry and it will be impractical for an international tribunal to conduct such an inquiry, concepts such as deference to national authorities and margin of appreciation have been applied.

A good faith review encompasses a certain degree of deference to the national authorities. Deference is a situation where the tribunal would acknowledge and respect the discretion of authorities to decide upon matters of public interest. Where a regulator operates in a specialized sector, an investment tribunal would not substitute its judgment and will give "certain degree of deference".[45] However, "such deference must not impede its task to verify whether international law was complied with. If there is any evidence that a decision taken by a regulator was abusive, did not afford due process or was

---

40 *Dispute Regarding Navigational and Related Rights (Costa Rica v Nicaragua)* [2009] ICJ Reports 213 (13 July 2009), para. 101.

41 *Philip Morris Brand SARL, Philip Morris Products S.A. and Abal Hermanos S.A. v. Oriental Republic of Uruguay*, ICSID Case No. ARB/10/7, Award (8 July 2016), paras. 135–141.

42 *Charanne and Construction Investments v. Spain*, SCC Case No. V 062/2012, Award (Unofficial English translation) (21 January 2016), paras. 513, 517.

43 *RREEF Infrastructure (G.P.) Limited and RREEF Pan-European Infrastructure Two Lux S.à r.l. v. Kingdom of Spain*, ICSID Case No. ARB/13/30, Decision on Responsibility and on the Principles of Quantum (30 November 2018), para. 460.

44 *El Paso Energy International Company v. The Argentine Republic*, ICSID Case No. ARB/03/15, Award (31 October 2011), para. 243.

45 *Marfin Investment Group Holdings S.A. and others v. Republic of Cyprus*, ICSID Case No. ARB/13/27, Award (26 July 2018), para. 899.

a pretense of form designed to conceal improper ends, a tribunal must find a breach of international law."[46]

States enjoy "wide regulatory space" in a certain context by relying on the nature of the State and the need to grant them deference. These tribunals acknowledge that a State can change its regulatory policies and the manner of their implementation based on "national views on public morals."[47] States deserve the discretion and deference towards that discretion because when States undertake actions, "some measure of inefficiency, a degree of trial and error, a modicum of human imperfection must be overstepped", otherwise every action by a State would be challenged before investment tribunals.[48] A tribunal does not have "an open-ended mandate to second-guess government decision-making".[49] The tribunal would grant a State, "a generous measure of appreciation, applied without the benefit of hindsight."[50] A tribunal should show 'deference' to the regulatory exercise of a State.[51]

Whenever there is an issue of exercise of discretion, it is practical to given a margin of appreciation.[52] Margin of appreciation is a tool devised by the ECtHR to check whether the measures of the State are compliant with the ECHR.[53] It means that States enjoy a certain degree of freedom while making choices and the judicial review would be exercised with restraint.[54] Investment tribunals have used the phrase "margin of appreciation" or "margin of freedom" are used to acknowledge the discretion of a State in adopting a regulatory measure. Although, it may not always be inspired by the case

46 *Marfin Investment Group Holdings S.A. and others v. Republic of Cyprus*, ICSID Case No. ARB/13/27, Award (26 July 2018), para. 900.

47 *International Thunderbird Gaming Corporation v. The United Mexican States*, UNCITRAL, Award, 26 January 2006, para. 127.

48 *Eastern Sugar B.V.(Netherlands) v. The Czech Republic*, Partial Award, SCC Case No. 088/2004 (27 March 2007), para. 272.

49 *S.D. Myers, Inc. v. Government of Canada, NAFTA Arbitration under the UNCITRAL Arbitration Rules* (2000), para 261; *Gemplus, S.A., SLP, S.A. and Gemplus Industrial, S.A. de C.V. v. United Mexican States*, ICSID Case No. ARB(AF)/04/3 & ARB(AF)/04/4, Award, (16 June 2010), para. 6.26.

50 *Gemplus, S.A., SLP, S.A. and Gemplus Industrial, S.A. de C.V. v. United Mexican States*, ICSID Case No. ARB(AF)/04/3 & ARB(AF)/04/4, Award, (16 June 2010), para. 6.26.

51 *Gemplus, S.A., SLP, S.A. and Gemplus Industrial, S.A. de C.V. v. United Mexican States*, ICSID Case No. ARB(AF)/04/3 & ARB(AF)/04/4, Award, (16 June 2010), para. 6.26.

52 *Invesmart v. Czech Republic*, UNCITRAL, Award (26 June 2009), para. 484.

53 See generally H Yourow, *The Margin of Appreciation Doctrine* (1993); Y Arai-Takashashi, *The Margin of Appreciation Doctrine and the Principle of Proportionality in the Jurisprudence of the ECHR* (2002).

54 William Burke-White & Andreas von Staden, "Private Litigation in a Public Law Sphere: The Standard of Review in Investor- State Arbitration" *Yale Journal of International Law* 35 (2010): 283, 304–308, 342–344.

law developed under the human rights framework. In *El Paso v Argentina*, the tribunal held that "Article XII grants an important margin of freedom to the host State in relation to its fiscal policy towards foreign investors, the States Parties indicate in paragraph 2 of Article XII that this policy should not be unfair or inequitable. Considering both the language used – "each Party should strive" – and the fact that Article XII (2) excludes, except in specific and limited cases, any review of a possible violation of the fair and equitable treatment standard, the Tribunal concludes that Article XII (1) creates only a best-effort obligation."[55] The position of the tribunal in *RREEF v Spain* was that "the Respondent enjoys a margin of appreciation in conducting its economic policy; therefore, it will not substitute its own views either on the appropriateness of the measures at stake or on the characterization of the situation which prompted them; in particular, the Tribunal will abstain to take any position on the issue of the existence of other or more appropriate possible measures to face this situation."[56] The noteworthy point is that it did not propose that it would investigate if there were alternative actions that the State ought to have taken. Margin of appreciation, however, is not unbridled. It does not give "unfettered discretion" to a State and the "discretionary" power or authority does not mean the freedom to act "arbitrary".[57]

In certain sensitive areas such as public health States would have greater margin of appreciation.[58] Where there are lethal effects on health greater deference would be given to the decision of the national authorities.[59] States have the discretion to adopt higher standards of protection than international standards due to the specific challenges that they face.[60] Sometimes it may not be possible to conduct detailed research before undertaking a regulation since some innovation may be necessary.[61] As long as the measure is

55 *El Paso Energy International Company v. The Argentine Republic*, ICSID Case No. ARB/03/15, Award (31 October 2011), para. 291.

56 *RREEF Infrastructure (G.P.) Limited and RREEF Pan-European Infrastructure Two Lux S.à r.l. v. Kingdom of Spain*, ICSID Case No. ARB/13/30, Decision on Responsibility and on the Principles of Quantum (30 November 2018), para. 468.

57 *RREEF Infrastructure (G.P.) Limited and RREEF Pan-European Infrastructure Two Lux S.à r.l. v. Kingdom of Spain*, ICSID Case No. ARB/13/30, Decision on Responsibility and on the Principles of Quantum, (30 November 2018), para. 468.

58 *Philip Morris Brand SARL, Philip Morris Products S.A. and Abal Hermanos S.A. v. Oriental Republic of Uruguay*, ICSID Case No. ARB/10/7, Award (8 July 2016), para. 399.

59 *Philip Morris Brand SARL, Philip Morris Products S.A. and Abal Hermanos S.A. v. Oriental Republic of Uruguay*, ICSID Case No. ARB/10/7, Award (8 July 2016), para. 418.

60 *Philip Morris Brand SARL, Philip Morris Products S.A. and Abal Hermanos S.A. v. Oriental Republic of Uruguay*, ICSID Case No. ARB/10/7, Award (8 July 2016), paras. 404–406.

61 *Philip Morris Brand SARL, Philip Morris Products S.A. and Abal Hermanos S.A. v. Oriental Republic of Uruguay*, ICSID Case No. ARB/10/7, Award (8 July 2016), para. 407.

in good faith and is reasonable whether or not actual results were achieved through resort to the measure is immaterial.[62]

States have produced evidence, such as scientific material to establish that the measure they adopted was in good faith.[63] There may not always be sufficient scientific information on a given matter. But certain effects are obvious and based on experience appropriate regulations may be adopted even in the absence of sufficient background information.[64] Therefore, it is not always possible to provide a rationally precise or perfect justification. Some flas such as "ill-conceived, counterproductive and excessively burdensome" in regulations may exist, for example say in legislations. But that does not mean that such regulations constitute breach of an investment treaty. As per the tribunal in *Paushok v Mongolia*:

> On the other hand, the fact that a democratically elected legislature has passed legislation that may be considered as ill-conceived, counterproductive and excessively burdensome does not automatically allow to conclude that a breach of an investment treaty has occurred. If such were the case, the number of investment treaty claims would increase by a very large number. Legislative assemblies around the world spend a good part of their time amending substantive portions of existing laws in order to adjust them to changing times or to correct serious mistakes that were made at the time of their adoption. A claim for a breach under an investment treaty has to be proven by claimants under the specific rules established in that treaty.[65]

---

62 *Philip Morris Brand SARL, Philip Morris Products S.A. and Abal Hermanos S.A. v. Oriental Republic of Uruguay*, ICSID Case No. ARB/10/7, Award (8 July 2016), paras. 409–410.

63 *Methanex Corporation v. United States of America*, UNCITRAL, Award, 3 (August 2005), Part III, Chapter A; Also see *Parkerings-Compagniet AS v. Republic of Lithuania*, ICSID Case No. ARB/05/8 11 September, Award, 11 September 2007, para 368; *Rumeli Telekom A.S. and Telsim Mobil Telekomunikasyon Hizmetleri A.S. v. Republic of Kazakhstan*, Award (29 July 2008), para 715; *Philip Morris Brands Sàrl, Philip Morris Products S.A. and Abal Hermanos S.A. v. Oriental Republic of Uruguay*, ICSID Case No. ARB/10/7, paras. 394, 400, 418–419.

64 *Crompton (Chemtura) Corp. v. Government of Canada*, PCA Case No. 2008-01, Award (2 August 2010), para. 135.

65 *Sergei Paushok, CJSC Golden East Company and CJSC Vostokneftegaz Company v. The Government of Mongolia*, UNCITRAL, Award on Jurisdiction and Liability (28 April 2011), para. 299.

CHAPTER 8

Conclusions

Exercise of regulatory freedom is essential and insensible for the modern State. With increasing challenges there would be more demand for regulations from various corners, including the need for innovative regulations. The presence of IIAs and the treatment standards therein, do not negate regulatory freedom. After initial trepidation, investment tribunals have found that regulatory freedom, if it satisfies certain parameters can be exercised without violating any of the treatment standards.

Regulatory freedom is protected because it is an inherent right of States. The right originates from sovereignty and it is a part of the central duty of the State to undertake regulations to protect public interest. States make and change regulations which may cause losses to the foreign investor without the responsibility to compensate provided the requirement of customary international law – in other words – the elements of regulatory freedom are satisfied.

Regulatory freedom is a rule customary international law. Conceptually, regulatory freedom flows from sovereignty since sovereignty is a multi-faceted concept of which regulatory freedom is a part. Additionally, regulatory freedom satisfies the requirements of a custom that is *opinio juris* and State practice. The evidence of *opinio juris* and State practice can be found in official statements of States, expressions of State practice, resolutions and participation in resolutions of international organizations, pleadings of States before international courts and tribunals, national legislations and constitutions, including decisions of national courts and the decisions of international courts and tribunals. Regulatory freedom has been recognized in various areas of international law despite a treaty covering a given field.

The act of entering into an IIA does not imply exclusion of regulatory freedom. Entering into IIAs is an exercise of sovereign authority whereby some aspects of sovereignty are parted but the remaining aspects continue to exist. Being a customary international law rule it co-exists along with the treaty obligation of treatment standards in IIAs. Therefore, regulatory freedom is not effaced, the manner of exercise of regulatory freedom is 'tapered'. The co-existence of regulatory freedom alongside treatment standards is supported by the principles governing the relationship of treaty and customs as sources of international law. There is no hierarchy between treaties and customs hence there is nothing to support the claim that the act of entering into IIAs excludes the application of customary international law rule of regulatory

 | DOI:10.1163/9789004759831_009

freedom. International courts and tribunals, including and particularly the ICJ have upheld this principle time and again. The only way in which regulatory freedom could be excluded by the treatment standards which are a treaty rule is if there is a clear exclusion of regulatory freedom or there is a conflict between the two.

There cannot be a presumption of conflict between regulatory freedom and treatment standards. Simply because a regulatory measure affects the foreign investor does not mean that the regulation falls in the same area of IIAs and is thereby the operation of regulatory freedom is excluded by treatment standards does not work conceptually and in practice. Both the norms, that is regulatory freedom and treatment standards have to be harmoniously interpreted to avoid any conflict. Conflict would arise if they are directly incompatible due to which compliance with one would result into violation of another. The nature and contents of regulatory freedom are such that it stands alongside treatment standards without overlapping or conflicting with them. Treatment standards such as expropriation, fair and equitable treatment and non-discrimination provisions such as MFN and NT support the absence of conflict. Presuming there is a conflict and the rule of *lex specialis* is applied, regulatory freedom would be the special rule. IIAs do not contain provisions on regulatory freedom and even where they are present, they are limited in scope. Regulatory freedom as a rule of customary international law provides a specialised set of rules that comprehensively regulate matters relating to regulatory freedom. Decisions of international courts and tribunals in various areas of international law affirm this point. They allow regulatory freedom to operate irrespective of the presence of a treaty obligation and the elements they identify are common to those reflected in *opinio juris* and State practice.

Interaction of treatment standards and regulatory freedom establishes the operation of regulatory freedom. The potential for overlap and conflict between indirect expropriation and regulatory freedom was posed by some of the early tribunals. But the trend changed in favour of allowing both to operate concurrently whereby regulatory freedom does not constitute breach of indirect expropriation. The tribunals that have declined to recognise regulatory freedom have done so due to the use of the sole effects doctrine. In situations of indirect expropriation, only the effect of the measure needs to be seen. The sole effects doctrine test was an outcome of the jurisprudence of the IUSCT where that tribunal had the jurisdiction to find a States responsible for all measures that affected property rights. The expropriation standard in IIAs, including indirect expropriation is not as broad as the such a broad as the IUSCT to include all measures affecting property rights. It is limited to prohibiting expropriatory measures, that is measure aimed at taking the property. In the case of regulatory freedom no taking takes place and the injury suffered is a result of the measure rather than the objective of the measure. Therefore, the assessment of the 'nature of measure', instead of its 'effect' is more important. The most appropriate approach is therefore to look at the nature of the measure – a practice that was applied by the PCIJ in the *Oscar Chinn* case and followed thereafter. The effect of this approach, as now followed by most investment tribunals is that regulatory freedom can be exercised without being perceived as indirect expropriation.

The fair and equitable treatment standard is a fact-based standard. Due to its flexibility tribunals have added several elements to it. These elements are used to check if the State has violated the fair and equitable treatment standard. Legitimate expectations of the foreign investor is one of the prominent elements developed in case law. As a preliminary requirement all expectations have to be legitimate or reasonable. It is not legitimate or reasonable to expect that States would not make or change laws, otherwise fair and equitable treatment would operate as a stabilization clause, which is not the intention behind IIAs. Legitimate expectations are to be seen in the overall context and it would not be fair to presume that the States relinquished their regulatory freedom and the investor so expected. An expectation that the regulatory freedom would not change does not arise unless there are specific assurances. Yet, these assurances cannot limit the freedom of States to make general regulations and exercise regulatory freedom to address serious concern of public interest. Stability of the legal framework is another element of fair and equitable treatment developed by investment tribunals and sometimes associated with legitimate expectations. Tribunals have clarified that stability of the legal framework is not an absolute rule and does not stifle regulatory freedom of States. The purpose of fair and equitable treatment standard is to investigate if the governmental actions are not arbitrary, discriminatory or unreasonable. The measures of a State shall be taken in good faith to protect public interest. For a measure to fall within the category of regulatory freedom, the first condition is that it shall be undertaken in good faith. Hence a measure satisfying the conditions of regulatory freedom cannot constitute a breach of the fair and equitable treatment standard. Also, regulatory freedom falls above the international minimum standard since the elements of regulatory freedom provide a higher threshold than the fair and equitable treatment standard. All the pertinent elements of fair and equitable treatment recognise the presence and operation of regulatory freedom. Therefore a measure satisfying the requirements of regulatory freedom does not violate fair and equitable treatment.

The elements of regulatory freedom are bona fide or good faith, non-discrimination, public interest and due process. These are parts of customary international law and identified by international courts and tribunals in various cases. Good faith is the most important elements since it is the decisive factor and influences other elements of regulatory freedom. The inquiry of good faith is to be done by looking at the background material. Good faith requires that the actions of States are not used to defeat the treaty obligations. Non-discrimination is influenced by non-discrimination provisions such as MFN, NT and fair and equitable treatment. Non-discrimination requires equal treatment of similarly placed entities. But there is no obligation of absolute equality. If there is supervening public interest and sound policy reasons there can be discrimination since sometimes discrimination is necessary to achieve equality. States have the discretion to choose the public interest they wish to preserve and the manner in which the wish to preserve, as long as these choices are not tainted by caprice or malice. Public interest will also change from one community to another and from time to time. While adopting a regulatory measure States have to adhere to due process. Since foreign investors are directly affected by measures of States it is necessary that due process is followed in the process of making and changing regulations. It is only when all these elements are satisfied that a measure will be an exercise of regulatory freedom and not constitute breach of treatment standards in IIAs.

The last but the important procedural question is the standard of review ought to be applied in matters of regulatory freedom. Necessity and proportionality have been applied by international courts and tribunals such as the WTO and ECtHR if there is support in the treaty text of the underling rule of customary international law. IIAs do not contain such provisions. The most appropriate standard of review in such situations, as applied by the ICJ is good faith or reasonableness review. The good faith test has two requirements: whether the objective of the measure is reasonable and if the steps taken to achieve the goal are reasonable. Investment tribunals often call the test they apply as the proportionality test, whereas in reality it is a good faith review.

Thus, States retain regulatory freedom despite entering into IIAs but the manner of that exercise is controlled by the requirements of customary international law. If those conditions are satisfied there is no breach of treatment standards.

www.ingramcontent.com/pod-product-compliance
Lightning Source LLC
Chambersburg PA
CBHW031327230926
51848CB00001B/129
* 9 7 8 9 0 0 4 7 5 9 7 6 3 *